How to RESPOND
WHEN YOUR HUSBAND
DOESN'T WANT SEX

I want him *to* want me

by **SHERI MUELLER**

FOCUS
ON THE FAMILY.

*A Focus on the Family resource
published by Tyndale House Publishers*

A Focus on the Family book published by Tyndale House Publishers, Carol Stream, Illinois 60188

Focus on the Family and the accompanying logo and design are federally registered trademarks of Focus on the Family, 8605 Explorer Drive, Colorado Springs, CO 80920.

Tyndale and Tyndale's quill logo are registered trademarks of Tyndale House Ministries.

Cover design by Sarah Susan Richardson

Interior illustration of pie chart provided by the author and drawn by Laura Cruise. Copyright © Focus on the Family. All rights reserved.

Unless otherwise indicated, all Scripture quotations are from The ESV® Bible (The Holy Bible, English Standard Version®), copyright © 2001 by Crossway, a publishing ministry of Good News Publishers. Used by permission. All rights reserved. Scripture quotations marked AMP are taken from the Amplified® Bible (AMP), copyright © 2015 by The Lockman Foundation. Used by permission. www.lockman.org. Scripture quotations marked MSG are taken from *The Message*, copyright © 1993, 2002, 2018 by Eugene H. Peterson. Used by permission of NavPress. All rights reserved. Represented by Tyndale House Publishers. Scripture quotations marked NASB are taken from the (NASB®) New American Standard Bible,® copyright © 1960, 1971, 1977, 1995, 2020 by The Lockman Foundation. Used by permission. All rights reserved. www.lockman.org. Scripture quotations marked NIV are taken from the Holy Bible, *New International Version,*® *NIV.*® Copyright © 1973, 1978, 1984, 2011 by Biblica, Inc.® Used by permission. All rights reserved worldwide.

The use of material from or references to various websites does not imply endorsement of those sites in their entirety. Availability of websites and pages is subject to change without notice.

For information about special discounts for bulk purchases, please contact Tyndale House Publishers at csresponse@tyndale.com, or call 1-855-277-9400.

ISBN 978-1-64607-077-0

Printed in the United States of America

30	29	28	27	26	25	24
7	6	5	4	3	2	1

Contents

Author's Note

OUT OF RESPECT FOR THE PRIVACY of clients and others who have shared their stories and entrusted me with their experiences, all stories in this book are composites—fictional accounts based on the experiences of many individuals. Similarities to any real person are coincidental and unintentional. However, my personal experiences shared within these pages are accurate and truthful, and they are fully approved by my loving and supportive husband.

This book is not intended as a therapy manual, nor is it intended to replace the advice of physicians or other licensed health professionals. Individual readers are solely responsible for their own physical or mental health care decisions and should consult a licensed professional in such matters. Neither the publisher nor I accept responsibility for any adverse effects individuals claim to experience, whether directly or indirectly, from the information contained in this book.

Acknowledgments

I FIRST WANT TO THANK MY HUSBAND, JIM. I tell everyone I meet that he is the love of my life. We met when I was fourteen, and ours has been a lifetime love story. Jim believes in me, encourages me, challenges me, and is a wise, handsome, wickedly funny, and Christ-honoring man. His prayers and spiritual guidance help keep me centered. Our daughters even remark, "Mom, you found a good one."

To my two beautiful, talented daughters, who are gifted in so many ways and have blessed us with five incredible grandchildren: You are my pride and my delight in life. Your expressions were priceless when I told you I was writing a book about sex, but both of you were proud of me for stepping out in faith to give a voice to other women. Yes, you may cover your ears—but not your eyes, since I want you to read this book someday.

To dear friends and family members who encouraged me, supported me, and helped me dream about writing this book to help Christian women: I love you. One dear friend lost a health battle during the creation of this book and now gets to dance with Jesus every day. As I typed the words in this book, I imagined her whispering in His ear quite often, saying, "Tell Sheri to go this way."

To my colleagues and spiritual brothers and sisters, who were always cheering me on and asking me how things were going: You inspired me to stick with this project even on days that were long, exhausting, and filled with tears—days when I was ready to consider the shredder. Your prayers kept me going.

To Karen Neumair, my literary agent, and the team at Credo Communications: You believed in this project from the beginning and walked beside me through some very trying moments. I am forever grateful.

To Jeff, the editor who stepped up to help me breathe: What a gift you've been!

Lastly, to my dear sweet Savior, Jesus Christ: Thank You for loving me and saving me. Without You, I would not be the woman I am today.

Introduction

THIS BOOK STARTED WITH ONE WOMAN—one woman who was brave and bold enough to contact me in response to an article called "Going Sexless." Her words were raw, direct, and filled with pain. She seemed astonished that there were other women like her with a husband who seldom participates in sex. She signed her email, "Needs Help."

Needs Help contacted me through the nonprofit ministry my husband and I founded in 2004 called Marriagetrac—an organization dedicated to transforming ordinary marriages into great marriages. The "Going Sexless" article had appeared in our Marriagetrac monthly e-newsletter, and it had apparently struck a nerve.

This is what Needs Help wrote:

Oh wow! I thought I was the only woman who feels this way! I get sick of reading or hearing from other women how much their men think about sex constantly and how much they want it because my husband is the total opposite. I have found pornography on his laptop, and he lies about it and shrugs it off as no big deal. I was blamed for looking at his

1

*history. We even went to counseling over this with our pastor
and it was completely looked over! It's so frustrating that
my husband gets to be this way, and I'm the one who hurts
deeply. I am a wife who is neglected sexually. He doesn't even
kiss me anymore.*

Her email was dated June 11, 2014. I had recently graduated with
a master's degree in professional counseling. I'd been running a
nonprofit by day and attending grad school at night. (Crazy, I
know!) I didn't know it at the time, but that was the day the seed
was planted for this book—and not just for this book, but also for
how God would teach, challenge, and grow me in the process of
working on it.

Today I am a full-time licensed counselor in private practice,
and I still serve part-time with Marriagetrac. The more I worked
with men and women daily in private practice, the more God
opened my eyes to the sexual-desire differences in almost every
marriage. As male and female, or even as husband and wife, we are
not wired to be completely in sync sexually. In fact, we are rarely
in sync—if ever. And that's okay. Men and women have differing
sex drives that God orchestrated as normal and beautiful, but our
world tends to twist and distort those differences into knots, an
issue that Needs Help made quite clear.

Needs Help is not alone. And if you resonate with her words,
neither are you. Since that initial email arrived in 2014, countless
other women—ranging in age from twenty-one to eighty-one—
have written to me begging for more Christians to talk about
how often husbands can and do refuse sex and reject their wives.
Furthermore, they want those who do address sexual-desire differences to please stop making blanket statements about how women
are always the ones to say no to sex and are somehow responsible
for almost every sexual issue in marriage. It's simply not accurate.

Many Christian women today suffer in silence. They endure virtually sexless marriages and desperately want someone to address this issue from their point of view—to provide another perspective. There is a recurring theme from the Christian women who dare to share their stories: *no more silence*. They are tired of being perceived as strange or abnormal just because they have a higher sex drive or because their husbands have virtually no sex drive at all. Why, they ask, is it so wrong for women to want more sex when it's entirely acceptable for men to feel this way?

I pray over every note or comment I receive. I've asked God numerous times, *What do you want me to do with this topic? Do you want me to tell these women's stories?* (God and I play a lot of tug-of-war!) The book you are holding is the answer to that question, and I hope the words you are about to read will honor the struggles of so many women who've been drowning in relationship pain for much too long.

In part 1 of this book, we'll address wives who wonder, *Why am I always the one to blame?* We'll look at why husbands aren't interested in or won't have sex, why some husbands don't "get it" and fail to understand their wives' higher libido, the mistaken notion that *wives* must be the problem, and the lies and assumptions we believe about sexual desire in men and women.

In part 2, we'll address what I call the real culprits, including physical or mental health, the issue of neurodiversity, husbands who meet their needs elsewhere, male insecurities, potential victimization, tendencies and interests that lie elsewhere, issues of control or abuse, and reasons a husband might not live up to expectations.

In part 3, we'll tackle potential solutions, such as making adjustments to previously unsuccessful strategies, considering how sexual differences are not *his* issue but perhaps *our* issue, and redefining intimacy.

In part 4, we'll consider where we go from here by embracing healthy sexuality, redefining intimacy, noticing our husbands' goodness, and no longer feeling alone as women who experience higher sexual desire. Finally, I've included an appendix, "A Message to Husbands"—a note of encouragement from my husband, Jim, to the men who want to hear a husband's perspective on the topic.

Please note that this book is *not* primarily addressed to those who are dealing with what I would call a normal desire discrepancy. Individual sex drives don't remain constant throughout the life of a marriage, and these fluctuations can become more pronounced the longer a couple is together. In other words, it's extremely rare for couples to desire equal amounts of sex at any given time.

Many couples seek counseling to help them work through these differences, and that's wonderful. Understanding what your spouse is thinking and feeling about sex—and how to communicate your thoughts and feelings—is a great skill to develop in marriage. So if you desire sex three times a week and your husband only wants it once a week, that's an important topic of discussion, but it's not the same as enduring weeks, months, or even years without any physical intimacy in your marriage. You can certainly benefit from the information in this book, but it was not written primarily for you.

This book is written especially for women like Needs Help—wives who feel neglected or even ignored by their husbands sexually. Yet none of what you'll read is intended to "bash" the lower-desire partner. My aim is to validate and illuminate the often-underrepresented challenges faced by women who are the higher-desire partner. I want to help you find God's best for *your* marriage—to help you learn to work together, lovingly and sacrificially, to attain the best sex life for you and your spouse. I won't tell you that it's easy, but I'll do my best to help you.

I want us to set aside any "battle of the sexes" mentality in pursuit of something far more beautiful—that is, the intimate knowing and listening to and learning from each other. Relying on outdated stereotypes, more than likely, will result in a losing battle. Instead, work to see your spouse as the one-of-a-kind individual you married. In other words, your mindset plays a vital role in fostering a kind and growing marriage.

Some chapters in this book are full of compassionate understanding, while others are about soul-searching and potentially uncomfortable challenges. One book obviously can't address every possible issue regarding desire differences, but what it can do is start the discussion—a discussion that's been long suppressed and seemingly off-limits for many (if not most) Christian wives. I've also included a bit about my own marriage experience.

So are you ready to get started? I view life as an adventure with God, and I expect He might take you on one while you read this book. Do not fear, for God is holding your hand. My prayers are with you as we journey on the healing road ahead.

PART ONE

The Problem:

"WHY AM I ALWAYS THE ONE TO BLAME?"

1

He Won't Have Sex with Me

TONIGHT'S THE NIGHT, YOU THINK. The kids are in bed, you've put away the evening's dinner dishes, and now you've set your sights on *dessert*. You've dabbed a bit of perfume on your pulse points and slipped into some alluring lingerie. The scented candles will provide just the right environment. In fact, you've done everything the so-called experts have suggested to help create a night of romance and passion.

You nestle in next to your sweetheart on the couch as he watches television. You quietly wait until commercial time, then you slide your hand over his arm and gently massage it.

With barely a look in your direction, he pulls back his arm, moves closer to the dog, and readjusts his position.

Not to be deterred, you take a breath and go in for a less subtle second attempt. "Hey, babe, the kids are asleep," you whisper. "What do you say we go upstairs and mess around?"

"Not tonight," he says, still not looking your way.

You can feel the tension in your shoulders as you sense this night ending as so many others have before. But still you press on, hoping that *this time* you'll get him to change his mind.

"Come on, babe. We haven't had sex in a while. I promise you'll enjoy it. Look what I'm wearing—just for you."

He finally glances your way and then back toward the television. If he noticed the lingerie, he's not letting on.

"I don't feel like it," he responds. "I just want to watch my show."

And there it hangs. Rejection. Again. You get up off the couch and head to your bedroom, where you blow out the candles and throw your lingerie in the garbage, telling yourself that this is the last time you want to feel this way. Then you sit on the bed, alone, as disappointment, frustration, anger, hurt, and a deep ache all flow over you.

Why doesn't he want me? you wonder. *What's wrong with me?* And the tears come again—as they have so many times before.

Since the dawn of recorded history, it feels like the predominant belief in the culture at large has been that men are the virile, testosterone-filled pursuers whose sex-switch is forever in the on position. Women, meanwhile, are portrayed as the ones who play hard to get, have an innately lower sex drive, and rarely have a need for their own sexual pleasure. But for many married women—as many as 30 percent of them—that perception isn't reality.[1] These women desire to be loved and cared for sexually and to have a healthy and passionate intimate relationship, yet they enter marriage and discover—either early on or later in the relationship— that their husband isn't all that interested.

These women aren't asking for anything outrageous or even out of the ordinary. They represent all ages, all seasons of marriage, and all backgrounds. They include devout Christian women and women who aren't quite sure about their faith. Some are newly wedded; others have been married for decades. The spectrum is wide indeed.

But these women all have this in common: They yearn to be loved intimately, to experience affection both in and outside the bedroom. They long for their husbands to notice them.

THE SECRET SHAME

From what I've learned about these women, most of them suffer in silence. A fear of being judged or misunderstood compels them to keep their secret hidden deep in their souls. For some, their situation feels so shameful that they don't share it even with their closest friends. How do you admit, "My husband has no sexual desire for me"? It certainly isn't something they announce on social media.

Why doesn't *he desire me?* they wonder.

Some men sit around with each other and complain, perhaps jokingly, that "my wife doesn't give me any." But you rarely catch a woman telling her friends, "My husband doesn't give me any." Why is that? I believe it speaks to our perception of our worth, our beauty, and who we are as women.

When these women *do* gather the courage to share, too often they receive uninformed responses that put the responsibility for the sexual success or failure of their marriages back on them: *Light some candles. Lose some weight. Seduce your husband. Be more submissive. Be more daring.* Many of these advice-givers mean well, but the message is little more than *If you just do x, y, and z, you'll please your husband and he will want to have sex with you.*

So these women obediently follow the advice . . . only to fail. They pray desperately for God to change their circumstances, but when their prayers aren't answered, the shame digs deeper and they determine to never again share the truth of their situation. Because they have no one to turn to, the cycle of shame continues and eats away at their self-esteem. Their marriages, their value as women, even their faith—all are at risk of becoming collateral damage.

In my work as a clinical counselor, as a marriage mentor for more than two decades, and through the marriage ministry at Marriagetrac.com, the number of women I've met who are struggling to be heard and wanted by their husbands is stunning. I've seen the devastating effects that sexual issues in marriage can have on a couple. Nowadays, more and more of those issues are related to differences in sexual desire.

I've received email after email and letter after letter from desperate women who are earnestly seeking a last chance at hope and help. When Marriagetrac tested the waters with a new article titled "I Want More Sex Than My Husband Does," it quickly became one of our most responded-to articles. It turned out that we'd given hurting women another invitation to share their stories, heartache, and pain.

Emails like these poured in:

I've begged and pleaded with my husband for twenty years. I've tried to understand from his perspective why he doesn't want me. I've finally given up, because the "hope" that something would change has destroyed me.

My husband and I have been married nine years and we have two daughters. But several years ago, he stopped wanting to have sex with me. I can't go on. I live like a virgin. I feel frustrated, hurt, disappointed, and starved. I thought I heard God tell me to marry this man, but why would God do this to me?

I've been married two years now and my husband's sex drive isn't there. We're both in our twenties! It hurts when other women say how much their husband wants sex, because that isn't the case with mine.

I'm ashamed to admit that my husband doesn't want to have sex with me. I don't know what I've done to turn him away, and he won't tell me. I feel so alone and ashamed. And to make matters worse, he's a pastor! So I feel even more alone—I certainly can't go to anyone in our church and say, "Help me. My husband won't have sex with me."

I was a virgin when I got married at the age of thirty-two. I dreamed of being intimate with my husband and experiencing sex the way God intended. Although we had sex on our wedding night, my husband has barely touched me since. We celebrate our twentieth anniversary next year. I love my husband, but I feel as though I've gotten ripped off. I waited— and for what?

I've heard from women who wonder why this is happening and how they can get through it. How can they love their husbands who reject them sexually? "Why is this my fault?" they ask, often immediately followed by the terrifying question "*Is* it my fault?" That's the shame they live with.

My heart broke for these women and what they were experiencing, but it wasn't until I found myself in a situation where I was the one with greater sexual desire than my husband that I truly understood the depth of frustration these women endure. I'll share more of my story in a later chapter, but I can personally attest to the discouragement, rejection, and loneliness that these women feel.

As for the experts' advice to just relax, take a bubble bath, light candles, make his favorite meal, lose a few pounds, wear lingerie, and give him pleasure first, it does nothing more than cement the message of *I'm to blame; obviously I'm flawed*. Not only is this misguided advice insulting, but it also damages women's souls.

YOU AREN'T ALONE

I'm assuming that if you've read this far, then you, too, have struggled with desire differences—or you know someone who has. By picking up this book, you've taken a step of faith, even if you feel like this is your last hope for any sort of change.

Right now I want to reassure you, to encourage you. As we journey through the following pages, take comfort in knowing that you are in a safe place. You will find no blame or judgments from me. As we explore the problems and the possible root causes, I hope you find the freedom to be open and transparent. I want you to recognize your worth as we discover together how to proceed with potential solutions that are about more than lighting candles and wearing alluring lingerie.

I realize that I'm repeating myself here, but it's vital for you to recognize that you aren't alone. The shame you've experienced may make you think you are, but many, many women—kind, God-honoring, Christian women—have dealt with or are dealing with the same desire differences as you. While the issues are all different to a degree, virtually all of these women have battled the blame-and-shame game. They get what you're feeling, and they get *you*. You're among friends here.

My heart aches that you and I and so many others have been hurt because of the prevailing messages about sex and sexuality. But now it's time to put to rest those messages that we've heard—and often believed—about ourselves and about marriage and sex.

It's time to put away the shame. I'll help you.

My dear reader, you also need to know something else, and it's extremely important: Your longing for touches, kisses, and hugs—and yes, sex with your husband—is a wonderful and natural thing. There is nothing wrong with wanting to be wanted. There is nothing wrong with wanting to be held and made love to. And you don't have to suffer in silence any longer.

> Shame is that warm feeling that washes over us, making us feel small, flawed, and never good enough.
>
> BRENÉ BROWN[2]

My Husband Doesn't Get It

ALLISON TOOK THE STEPS two at a time as she rushed upstairs to their bedroom. She flung herself onto the bed, pounded her fists into a pillow, and wept. This was supposed to be the room where Allison and her husband would enjoy the pleasures of sexual intimacy. But after two years of marriage, they'd experienced those pleasurable moments only a few times—and only when he initiated, which was rare.

She'd always believed the messages from her church, parents, and friends—that as a good Christian woman, she should let her husband initiate sex. But after months of abstinence, she couldn't understand why he didn't. She'd dropped hints that she was a ready and willing partner, but those hints seemed to fall on deaf ears. She eventually decided to be the initiator.

When her husband openly rejected her, saying he was too tired,

Allison gathered her hope and decided to try again when he was fresh. But still he said no, always offering some excuse that, frankly, seemed lame. Though she continued to hope that things would get better, the months wore on and nothing changed.

Talking openly about sex wasn't something Allison felt comfortable with, but she finally concluded that she needed to communicate both her feelings and her frustrations.

Maybe he says no all the time because I haven't actually communicated my desires to him—that I want *to have sex with him,* she rationalized to herself. *Maybe if I just help him understand that, then he'll get it.*

Allison waited for what she believed was the perfect moment. Her husband was in a good mood, they were interacting easily and enjoying the day, so she brought it up. Though she was nervous, she tried to state her case logically and clearly—only to be shut down immediately.

"Why are you constantly harassing me about this?" he asked her angrily. "Seriously! I don't want to talk about it. Why are you making it such a big deal?"

When Allison eventually tried again to state her case—that other husbands were eager to have sex with their wives—she was met with a snide comment: "Who are you comparing me to?"

Now Allison lay alone on their bed, feeling lonelier, more rejected, and more hopeless than she'd ever felt before.

She'd mistakenly believed that if she could somehow get through to him, then things would be different, that her husband would change. *I desire sexual fulfillment. How can he believe that I don't need it? I do!* She hit her pillow again. *If only he could understand what I'm feeling!*

Have you been there?

The problem isn't only that many husbands don't want sex, it's that they fail to understand why that's a problem for their wives.

Just like plenty of wives, many husbands (including Christian husbands) believe false narratives about women and their desire levels—narratives that usually begin with "Good, godly women don't . . ." This false mindset reduces the issue to the wife's problem: "Other women don't need sex as often, so why do you?" these men ask.

In turn, many wives don't know how to approach or communicate with their husbands effectively. They wish their husbands would simply "get it," but wishing won't solve this problem.

NO APOLOGIES NEEDED

Before we proceed, I need to state a simple truth: Some husbands don't understand their wives' desires because they don't *want* to understand. It's easier for them to justify not wanting sex by placing the blame on their wives.

Have you ever heard comments like these?

- "Good" women don't pursue their husbands for sex.
- Wives who want sex more than their husbands have a problem.
- Why is she so obsessed with sex?
- She was raised by her father, so she isn't feminine.
- She doesn't let me be the pursuer.
- I don't need sex, and I'm a man. She shouldn't need it either.
- She never wanted it so much before. Why now all of a sudden?
- She just needs to back off.

Rather than owning one's own issues, it's easier to find fault with a wife who is merely asking for what her heart and body crave within the union of marriage.

"The apostle Paul says not to withhold or deprive each other of sex except for a period of fasting and prayer, but my whole marriage has been one big, long fast, and I'm starving!" one woman told me with tears in her eyes. "When I try to express my frustrations and explain that what I want is good, my husband stomps away and refuses to speak to me. On the rare occasion that I get a response, I'm accused of exaggerating the issue. But I'm not . . . am I?"

No, this wife *isn't* being overly dramatic. She's simply asking to be loved by and intimate with the man she chose to spend the rest of her life with.

I've talked with women who are so confused and hurt by their husbands' lack of understanding that they *apologize* for feeling this way—wondering if they are somehow exaggerating the issue and comparing their husbands with the men they see in movies, on television, and on social media.

After all, numerous cultures and churches have long suggested that women are the less interested sexual parties in the marital relationship. If women want more sex, they must be smoldering temptresses or even "Jezebels." They have promoted the message that women should never pursue men, even their husbands, sexually.

Some readers of this book might have grown up in a culture that suggested women were responsible for making men lust, even though Jesus clearly stated it is a man's responsibility not to lust (see Matthew 5:28). Some women were told that they should never even acknowledge having any sexual desires prior to marriage. Compare that with how the message rapidly shifted after marriage: Once wed, they were told to be ever eager and willing to meet their husband's desires, once again to keep him from having lustful thoughts or being tempted to seek pleasure outside of marriage. In this view, *his* pleasure and his thoughts took priority over his wife's. Pleasing herself through marital sex might even be viewed as selfish or inappropriate.

Thankfully, this teaching has lost favor in recent years, but it hasn't disappeared completely. Some Christian women are still confused about whether it's okay to feel sexual desire, much less act on it.

As these women were taught, sexual desire leads to immodesty and the potential for immorality. So if a wife has a stronger sexual desire, then something must be wrong with *her*, right?

Wrong.

The "something must be wrong with her" mindset is an inherently distorted belief about women, one that compels us to light a match and blow this concept to smithereens. This thinking suggests that the sexual well-being or sexual decay of a marriage lies entirely at the wife's feet. Husbands are absolved of any responsibility. Yet a wife should never have to apologize for wanting to have a regular and mutually satisfying sexual relationship with her husband.

God created both men *and* women to be sexual beings. In fact, women have more sexual arousal spots on their bodies than men. I love that God designed us that way! Humans are one of only a few mammals in which the females experience orgasm. We desire sex not only for reproduction, but also long after childbearing years. Many women enjoy sex even more after children leave the nest.

This isn't some fluke. God *designed* women that way. We can't turn off those desires; we're wired for them. Sexuality is a gift that God has given us. As author Philip Yancey says,

> Having studied some anatomy, I marvel at God laboring
> over the physiology of sex: the soft parts, the moist
> parts, the millions of nerve cells sensitive to pressure
> and pain yet also capable of producing pleasure, the

intricacies of erectile tissue, the economical and ironic combination of organs for excretion and reproduction, the blending of visual appeal and mechanical design. . . . When I experience desire, I need not flinch in guilt, as if something unnatural has happened. Rather, I should follow the desire to its source, in search of God's original intent. . . . We cannot simply compartmentalize sexual desire.[1]

Arousal and desire don't apply only to husbands, but to wives as well. Women were created to enjoy and crave sex too. No wife need apologize for, regret, or feel disheartened over wanting what she has been wired for.

IT ISN'T JUST ABOUT THE SEX

Desire differences for women are about far more than just the sexual act. What a husband might not understand is that sex, for his wife, is much more than a physical connection; it is a heart-to-heart emotional connection. Women want to feel desired. So when husbands reject, make excuses, and even blame, wives don't view those interactions as isolated incidents. Those moments cut to the very core of their souls.

The message is sent that these women aren't *enough*—aren't good enough, valuable enough, engaging enough, beautiful enough. What else is a wife supposed to think? After all, the person they have vowed to love and honor till death do them part doesn't seem as interested in loving and honoring them back. When a husband doesn't want to be intimate with his wife, the feelings of blame and humiliation eventually carry over into the rest of their relationship.

I've mentored and counseled couples in which the husband

says sex isn't that important to him. "I don't desire porn—that isn't it," one said. "Sex just isn't at the top of my priority list." Whether he realized it or not, what message was he sending his wife? *Sex isn't a priority for me, so it shouldn't be a priority for you, either. Stop asking. I'm here, I work, I buy you things. Isn't that enough?*

That's the thinking of many men who have a lower sexual drive. Because they aren't all that interested, they expect their wives to feel the same way. They're surprised—and eventually annoyed—that their wives actually are interested. Remember, sex isn't *just* an act—it's about nurturing an engaged emotional relationship.

When the lower-desire partner is consistently apathetic about having sex with their spouse (whether male *or* female), they are in essence telling their spouse, *I'm not really that interested in this relationship.* That is understandably devastating to their spouse *and* to the marriage.

HOW DO I GET HIM TO UNDERSTAND?

Just as Allison believed, wives who encounter this desire disconnect hold on to the hope that if their husbands could better understand their feelings, then their husbands would change. They do everything they can think of to help their husbands "get it." They try to talk, only to be shut down. They grieve, only to be ignored. They pester and plead, only to be labeled as difficult. They withdraw, only to see nothing change . . . except for the increase in their pain. After all, how do they get their husbands to understand that, ultimately, wives can get nearly all their needs fulfilled outside the marriage—all except for sex?

If women need comfort, they can seek it outside the marriage. If they need advice, they can go outside the marriage. If they need to be cheered up or spiritually encouraged, they can call on friends, family, neighbors—even strangers at church or in community support groups. Yet to feel loved and valued through sexual intimacy, they have only one option—the marital relationship that God designed.

But where can they go for understanding when that sexual relationship is broken? For most Christian women, the answer is nowhere. How can a wife share the secret pain of her experience? If the secret got out, she knows it would only reflect poorly on her, not on her husband, and that makes her feel even more desperate and alone. To talk about one's sex life with others—especially those you might see at church? It just isn't done!

So how *do* we get husbands to understand our need? How do we move beyond pride and blame? The solution begins, at least in part, with us better understanding the underlying issues men experience. Even more so, it begins with us.

Marriage, of course, is based on give-and-take. Over the lifetime of a marriage, there will be times when each partner—husband and wife—might not be interested in physically making love for any number of emotional or physical reasons. (We joke about "having a headache," but it really can be hard to enjoy sex when your head is pounding.) We make sacrifices for each other when this is the case.

Keep in mind, however, that in this book we're talking about well-worn patterns that hardly ever budge. When this is the norm in a marriage, the hurt and frustration is like a low-grade fever that never seems to break—especially for the wife who desires sex and intimacy with a chronically unresponsive husband. That is why I must emphasize the following in the clearest terms possible:

There's nothing wrong with wanting intimacy, and whether your husband ever "gets it"—or if he gets it but chooses not to respond—you need not believe that you are somehow at fault when you ask for something that God created for your marital good and relational pleasure.

I Must Be the Problem

HANNAH STARED DOWN at the tissue she was holding, nervously gripping it until it began to disintegrate in her hands. "I haven't shared this with anyone else," she admitted, her voice soft and tight with emotion. "It's too . . ."

I sat quietly as she searched for the words I could have easily provided.

Shameful.

Embarrassing.

Humiliating.

Painful.

Slowly, Hannah told me about her sexless marriage, how her husband didn't seem interested, and how desperately she wanted to feel loved and cherished. She'd kept this secret for more than a decade.

"A few months ago, I went to a weekend get-together with some of my college friends," Hannah told me. "They all talked and laughed about how their husbands have one-track minds in their desire for sex. Deep down, I felt like my heart was being stabbed over and over."

"How did you respond when they talked that way?" I asked, already sensing the answer.

"I laughed and nodded, as though I had the same kind of husband." She paused as she sniffed. "I just couldn't tell them the truth. How could I admit that my husband has no desire for me? What would they think of me?"

This is the heart of the shame that so many wives endure. *What would they think of me? In other words, I must be the problem.*

For far too many of us and for far too long, we have embraced the belief that something is wrong with us for wanting intimacy—as though we need to apologize for *wanting* to be sexual beings.

It's time to embrace a different belief: that the burden isn't ours, and that we are not at fault. But it can be difficult to embrace a new belief, especially when the current belief is connected to a false narrative.

FALSE NARRATIVES WE BELIEVE ABOUT OURSELVES

Throughout our lives, our families, friends, and faith impress certain messages on us. Many of us were taught a false message that being sexually pure also meant being uninterested in sex, non-initiators . . . you get the point. We often embraced those messages without question, prayerful consideration, or Bible study, and they became part of who we are—what we call *narratives*.

A narrative is simply a story, but not all stories are true. Stories not based in fact are *false narratives*, and the notion that good Christian women shouldn't desire sex is definitely a false narrative. So is the notion that all men want sex all the time.

Narratives like these shape our identities as sexual women. They are ingrained into our past, present, and future. Believing these false narratives only reinforces our feelings of isolation and rejection, leaving us even more hopeless than before. And when feelings of rejection, fear, inadequacy, and loneliness take hold, we begin to listen to the condemning voices that tell us we are to blame for our husbands' lack of desire.

This often plays itself out in our minds through if/then/so thinking. It usually goes something like this . . .

If *I were (a better wife, lover, friend), and* **if** *I were (more daring, sensitive, alluring),* **then** *he (would pursue me, wouldn't withhold sex from me).* **So** *I must be the problem.*

If a husband is using porn, having affairs, dealing with physical or mental health issues, or just making excuses for not wanting to have sex, where does the ownership for that couple's sex life often fall? At the wife's feet. It comes back to this thinking: *I'm the problem. If he loved me enough, if he respected me enough, if he wanted me enough, if he whatever enough, then he would want me.*

This endless cycle of if/then/so doesn't get us any closer to what we want—which is intimacy, love, and, yes, pleasure. It keeps us stuck in shame and blame, believing that sex is conditional and we're at fault for not doing enough to entice and satisfy our men. This is where false beliefs about our sexuality can wreak havoc. Our minds start repeating certain ideas we've been taught and have embraced about ourselves, and those false narratives torment us. Sex counselor and psychotherapist Ian Kerner calls the results of these narratives a "compass of shame."[1]

It goes something like this:

Withdrawal

"I am sexually broken. I've given up on sex. I deserve whatever happens."

Attack Self

"What's wrong with me? Why am I such a loser? I guess I should just suck it up and stop pursuing sex."

Attack Other

"I'm interested in sex, but my partner has no concept of romance or foreplay. Most of the time he just ignores me. It's all that disgusting porn he watches!"

"Sex is overrated. Who has time for sex? Anyway, all couples stop having sex at some point."

Avoidance

First, we attack the other person. We think, *What's wrong with him? I'm a ready and willing partner, but he can't see how much I want to be intimate with him. He has no concept of romance or foreplay and just ignores me. It's all that disgusting porn he watches!* (Or whatever excuse we give him.)

Second, we begin to avoid. Our avoidance plays out via that internal voice: *Sex is overrated anyway. Who has time for sex? I'm way too busy. Anyway, all couples stop having sex at some point.*

Third, we move into attacking ourselves. We wonder, *What's wrong with me? Why am I such a loser? Isn't there something I can do to make him want me? I guess I should just give up and stop pursuing sex.*

Finally, we withdraw. Our false narrative tells us, *I am sexually broken; I am the problem. I deserve whatever happens.*[2]

The words vary from person to person, but the themes are remarkably similar. *I'm not beautiful. I'm not sexy. I'm not desirable. I'm not wanted. There's a deficit in me. There's a flaw in me. I'm not doing it right. I'm not giving him what he needs. If I can't fix it, I'm not worth it.*

These thoughts take up residence deep within us. *What did I do wrong? I must be the one who has the problem.*

HOW FALSE NARRATIVES DERAIL US

"What's the use in trying anymore?" Ruth said, wiping the tears from her eyes. "There's something wrong with me. No matter what I do, I can't make it right. I'm worthless."

It didn't matter that the woman sitting in front of me was a successful businesswoman, highly respected throughout the community and in her church. All Ruth knew at that moment were the false narratives she had embraced. It doesn't take much rejection from our husbands before we are off and running, our thoughts filled with lies about our beauty and self-worth.

RESPONDING TO OUR FALSE NARRATIVES

Phoebe walked confidently up to me and smiled. She'd been a part of our marriage ministry for years, but she and her husband had moved away several years ago for a job reassignment. She was back in town to visit family and stopped by to see me.

She and her husband had struggled with his porn addiction, and it had negatively affected all aspects of their relationship, including the sexual.

"You look good," I said. "How is your marriage?"

"Better," Phoebe replied, "though we're still recovering from his addiction. It's a long, slow process."

"I understand."

"Sheri, I wanted to thank you for something you did for me."

"Oh?" I raised my eyebrows. "What was that?"

"For many years of my marriage, I believed something was terribly wrong with me because of my husband's addiction," Phoebe explained. "I tried everything to make him desire me. And when I couldn't, I fell apart. I believed I was worthless. I believed the lies that said I had failed and was not a real woman or a good enough wife. But you reminded me that God created me as an exquisite sexual being, and that I never had to be ashamed about wanting my husband's affection and desire. You reminded me that I wasn't worthless."

"You aren't," I agreed.

She nodded. "I know. I finally, really know that now. It wasn't until I had a come-to-Jesus moment and surrendered my insecurities that I really began to see myself as God sees me: beautiful and worthy of a marriage that is healthy."

Tears came to her eyes, and she didn't wipe them away. "For the first time," she continued, "I really embraced the truth of who I am in Christ. It's made all the difference in how I see myself."

When we believe the falsehoods we've heard, we forget how the Lord sees us. God, our heavenly Father, loves us deeply, lavishly (see 1 John 3:1).

When we're tempted to believe *I'm not beautiful*, Scripture tells us that we are "fearfully and wonderfully made" (Psalm 139:14).

When we think, *I'm not desirable*, God's Word says, "I am my beloved's, and his desire is for me" (Song of Solomon 7:10).

When we think, *I'm not wanted*, the Bible says, "We love because he first loved us" (1 John 4:19).

And the most heartbreaking one is when we think, *This is what*

I deserve. God is punishing me for my past. However, Scripture says, "[Christ] took the punishment, and that made us whole. Through his bruises we get healed" (Isaiah 53:5, MSG). I've known strong Christian women who have suffered needlessly because of this false narrative.

I ask them, "If God is punishing you by making your husband avoid sex with you, what exactly is He punishing you for?"

An acquaintance once shared that during her college days one of her professors was sexually inappropriate with her, and she had done nothing to stop it. Now living in a sexless marriage, she wondered if God somehow gave her husband less desire because of what happened to her as a college student.

If you are holding on to this lie—that you have done something so deeply displeasing to the Lord that He has taken from you the sexual aspect of your marriage—then I encourage you to remember that when we come into relationship with God, He blots out our transgressions and no longer remembers our sins (see Isaiah 43:25). He is a God of grace (see John 1:16). He doesn't act in opposition to His own character.

When you find yourself thinking that you must be the cause of your husband's choices, I'd encourage you to stop and ask yourself:

- How am I attacking the person that God created me to be?
- What is it I believe about myself that leads to that attack?
- Do those beliefs line up with what Scripture says about who I am?

As you work to replace the false narratives you've believed, many thoughts and feelings will likely surface. You need to honestly consider these thoughts. Are they true? If you aren't sure, ask God to show you the truth about who you are and how He thinks of you. Pick up your Bible and start reading. Let the words of Scripture combat the lie that you are the problem in your sexless marriage. Find passages that give you comfort, then keep going back to them. I've known women who write verses on sticky notes and place them in their bathrooms, in their kitchens, and even in their cars.

Need a few passages to help you get started? Consider these:

- "I praise you, for I am fearfully and wonderfully made. Wonderful are your works; my soul knows it very well" (Psalm 139:14).
- "Fear not, for I have redeemed you; I have called you by name, you are mine" (Isaiah 43:1).
- "I have loved you with an everlasting love; therefore I have drawn you out with kindness" (Jeremiah 31:3, NASB).
- "Are not two sparrows sold for a penny? And not one of them will fall to the ground apart from your Father. But even the hairs of your head are all numbered. Fear not, therefore; you are of more value than many sparrows" (Matthew 10:29-31).

When you hear a negative voice whispering in your mind, *I am unloved, I am unlovable, I am the problem*, reach for your Bible and examine the evidence—because examining the evidence reveals distortions and lies.

It's time to stop placing the blame at your own feet. It's time to stop believing the false narratives that others have told you. It's time to embrace the beauty and the gift of your sexuality—of biblical womanhood—that God has given you.

> **What gives me the most hope every day is God's grace; knowing that his grace is going to give me the strength for whatever I face, knowing that nothing is a surprise to God.**
>
> RICK WARREN[3]

4

The Lies and Assumptions We Believe

"I COULDN'T HAVE BEEN MORE SURPRISED," said Mandy, tears flowing freely down her cheeks. She had been married for three years now, and married life wasn't what she had expected.

"I saved myself for thirty years, dreaming of the day when my husband wouldn't be able to take his hands off me. And what do I get instead? A man who isn't interested in sex as often as I am. How can that be possible? All men are sex starved, right? At least that's what I've always been told—that they have one-track minds."

"Who told you that?" I asked.

"Everybody! My married girlfriends, my sister, the movies, even my pastor. Everybody knows that's true," said a still-sobbing Mandy.

I waited a few moments for her to compose herself.

"What if it isn't true?" I asked.

She stared at me blankly. "What do you mean?"

"What if I told you that's a lie?"

Mandy shook her head. "But . . ." She paused, as though taking in the significance of what I'd just suggested. "Why would all those people lie?"

"They don't know they're lying," I said.

We've already looked at the false narratives we believe about ourselves. But what about the falsehoods and assumptions we've bought into about men, sex, and romance?

Take a moment to consider what you've been told about how men "should" behave or what "normal" sex is. Do any of the following sentiments sound familiar?

- Men have one-track minds. They are always ready to have sex, and their desire is unwavering.
- Men will take advantage of almost any sexual opportunity that presents itself.
- Men operate like a light switch: You can turn them on instantly.
- Men have more intense sexual desires than women.
- Men are like microwaves, and women are like slow cookers.
- Men are supposed to be the sexual initiators.
- Men's desires are triggered by superficial visual and physical cues.
- Sex for men is primarily about their own pleasure.
- Wives—especially Christian wives—need to "do their duty" and fulfill their husbands' needs whenever they want sex.
- "Normal" sexual activity is *at least* once a week, if not more.
- Sex that doesn't end in an orgasm isn't really good sex.
- "Normal" men look at pornography, and it does not harm their marriages.

You can probably add a few more of your own. These worn-out clichés are so prevalent in our culture—even in our churches—that we reflexively accept them as true. I've heard both Christian and non-Christian comedians joke about these assumptions. Pastors and marriage-seminar presenters cite them straight from the podium as if they were factual. If I had a nickel (another cliché!) for every time I've heard one of these tired platitudes, I'd have retired long ago.

I recently heard a well-known pastor preach a sermon on hope for hurting marriages. I *think* he was joking when he told his audience, "Men have a supernatural gift for making anything sexual. I rotate the tires. That's sexual. I'm ready to go. Unload the dishwasher. Ready to go."

But here's the truth: The pastor who claimed he could unload the dishwasher and be ready to have sex? If you asked him privately whether that's always the case, he'd likely confess that, no, it was an exaggeration to make a point in a lighthearted way—an opportunity for the congregation to have fun with his message.

No, men don't *always* make everything sexual. What the pastor failed to understand is that he was, perhaps unintentionally (I'm extending grace), helping cement those beliefs in his audience, unknowingly adding to the pain of many women. I imagine there were women in the congregation who wanted to ask, "If there are any husbands in the room who are not turned on by rotating tires and unloading dishwashers, please raise your hands. I need to know that my husband is not the only one."

Messages like these unknowingly promote confusion, isolation, and despair, furthering the belief that wives have no safe place to share their experiences and pain.

What's more, these messages continue to make things worse. These statements you've heard (and probably accepted at face value)? Author and clinical psychologist Juli Slattery calls them long-held cultural paradigms that are nothing more than assumptions—assumptions often presented to Christ-followers as fact. "The world is watching and laughing as Christians who worship the same God and read the same Bible can't agree on God's intention for sexuality," Slattery says. "We can't guide others if we ourselves are lost."[1]

These unhelpful thinking patterns, which counselors call cognitive distortions (*shoulds* and *musts* are typical examples), have devastated many couples—and their sex lives. They make us feel worse about ourselves, and they tend to provoke anxiety and depression. *Shoulds* and *musts* convey messages of shame and can be used as verbal forms of control. Though *some* people have learned to dismiss *some* of those thought patterns, countless others simply don't know better.

THE "SHOULDING" THAT HAPPENS

A sure giveaway that a statement is an assumption is the blatant—or sometimes underlying and unspoken—"shoulding" that happens: A man *should* be the pursuer. A wife *should* have the lower libido. Other word giveaways: *must, need to, ought to,* and *supposed to.*

What so many people fail to realize is that "shoulding" often equates to shaming. *You're my wife, so you must . . . You're my husband, so you ought to . . .* And because you aren't doing what a godly spouse *should*, you supposedly aren't a "real" man or woman. In other words, when I hear *shoulds*, I rarely hear grace.

As Christians, we can even twist Scripture into "shoulding." Consider two passages that are sometimes used to manipulate:

Wives, submit to your own husbands, as to the Lord.

EPHESIANS 5:22

Do not deprive one another, except perhaps by agreement for a limited time, that you may devote yourselves to prayer; but then come together again, so that Satan may not tempt you because of your lack of self-control.

1 CORINTHIANS 7:5

When we separate these passages from grace, they can become weapons to shame or control our spouses. When separated from grace, both verses can take on a different dynamic. The Ephesians passage can become a selfish demand that suggests "Submit to *me* . . . as to the Lord." However, demanded sex is not love. It does not show grace. Instead, it is coercive and potentially abusive. What the other spouse likely hears is *You should submit to me in all things, including the bedroom.*

We shouldn't neglect the verse directly preceding the Ephesians 5:22 direction to wives, which is also a clear directive: "Submit to *one another* out of reverence for Christ" (Ephesians 5:21, NIV, emphasis added). A Christian wife is to submit to her husband as a husband is to submit to his wife—not only because they respect, honor, and love each other, but because of their mutual devotion to Jesus. It ultimately comes back to our relationship with and love for Christ.

The 1 Corinthians verse can also be used as a selfish demand: *You don't get to deny me. The Bible says so!* Without an attitude of grace, we can end up shaming our spouses with the message *By not fulfilling my needs sexually, not only are you not a good spouse, you aren't a good Christian.* And that's extremely dangerous territory to enter.

Now that we've discussed some ways people can misuse Scripture, let's unpack some popular myths about sex and desire.

Myth 1: Men Are Always Ready to Have Sex

This is probably the greatest misconception we have embraced—that men are always ready and willing to have sex. A man in the movies or on television can endure a brutal beating that results in his eyes swollen shut, knife slashes all over his body, and multiple bullet wounds—injured to the point that he's barely alive. But an attractive woman shows up, and—wonder of wonders—our hero miraculously musters the strength to have sex with her! I always laugh during those scenes. *Really?* I think. This is fantasy to the most insane degree.

"Well, yes, Sheri, I know—but that's the imaginary world of movies and TV," you say. And I agree—but those messages still sink in. We somehow believe that it can work that way in real life, too.

Nobody is always ready to have sex. Let me say that again so you can sit with it for a moment: *Nobody* is always ready to have sex. I would be terrified to undergo a serious surgery if I knew that my surgeon was just one thought away from wanting to have sex. "Scalpel," he says to his medical assistant. And as he makes an incision, he thinks, *Hmmm, too bad my wife isn't here. I'm in the mood.* It's ridiculous.

Think about it. While you might have a higher libido than your husband, you aren't in the mood all the time either, right?

So why do we think men are ready to head for the bedroom at a moment's notice? This stereotype is insulting and degrading, especially to men. Intentionally or not, we've labeled them as being unable to control themselves sexually. As biblical scholar David Clines wrote in a chapter called "David the Man: The Construction of Masculinity in the Hebrew Bible," one of the great demands on men is to "be sexual. Men are supposed to be sexually experienced, and to be always interested in sex."[2] And in *Gendered Lives: Communication, Gender, and Culture*, author and professor Julia T. Wood explained, "Sex isn't a free choice when you have to perform to be a man."[3]

Yet this myth prevails. Perhaps it stems from the idea that testosterone is the great sexual motivator. But consider this: Testosterone levels are at their highest in most men somewhere between the ages of eighteen and twenty—in other words, during the transition from late adolescence into early adulthood. After that, it's all downhill. Testosterone levels decrease as men age, by as much as 1 percent per year after the age of thirty. So unless your husband is a teenager, it's likely that he won't *always* be focused on having sex. (And not even all teenage boys are that way!)

If your husband is sixty, that means his testosterone levels have decreased by an average of about 30 percent from his peak.[4] (This is a generalization, of course. Every man's testosterone level is different depending on many different factors, such as age, health, and family history.) Testosterone levels can fluctuate from day to day and even throughout the day. They typically peak in the morning, and then diminish throughout the day. Once again, those fluctuations will differ for individuals.[5]

If you find yourself frustrated because you're in the mood at bedtime yet your husband isn't interested, might knowing about his fluctuating testosterone levels affect your frustration and shift your heart toward compassion?

After all, we women know that we have ebbs and flows in our desire. When we're stressed, exhausted, overworked, fearful, sad, angry, or experiencing any number of situations, we might not be interested in having sex. If that's true of us, why would we think that the same thing isn't true of our husbands?

In fact, studies show that stress is just one potential silent killer of a couple's sex life.[6] A 2019 study published by BodyLogicMD found that 51 percent of respondents admitted to "dead bedrooms"—sexless relationships—because of work-related stress.[7]

So if your husband has a high-stress job and a low sex drive, could it be possible that the culprit is stress? If he's anxious or worried or under pressure, that can affect his sex drive. Exhaustion can also affect his sex drive.

There's a well-known movie scene that illustrates this reality. It appears in *Raiders of the Lost Ark*.

If you're looking for a so-called man's man in the movie world (at least in the early 1980s), look no further than Indiana Jones, played by a virile Harrison Ford. In the movie, Indy has been injured in a fight. He's slashed, bruised, and beaten. As the love interest, Marion, is tending to his wounds, Indy grimaces and complains that everywhere she tries to soothe him hurts.

"Where *doesn't* it hurt?" she finally asks. He points to his elbow, which she kisses. Next he points to his forehead and tells her, "Here." So she kisses him there. He points to his eyelid, and then finally to his lips. The passion mounts as they begin to kiss, the music swells, and then . . . he falls asleep. Though the moment is humorous, there's a lot of truth in it. Husbands might want to be in the mood, but their bodies don't always cooperate. That doesn't mean they are less than "real" men, because all men experience times of decreased testosterone or simple exhaustion.

As we consider this myth, a good question to ask and then contemplate comes from a leading relationship therapist and researcher on sexual desire. In her book *Not Always in the Mood*, Sarah Hunter Murray asks, "Is sexual desire allowed to change over time?"[8]

According to the mistaken assumption that men are always ready, the answer would be no. But if sexual desire can shift from day to day—or even hour to hour—how might that knowledge gradually impact your self-perceptions, your beliefs about yourself, and your beliefs about your husband?

Murray goes on: "It is completely normal for a man's interest to ebb and flow and for him to not want to have sex even when you're interested. This isn't cause for pain, it's just normal human experience and variation. Further, most often when men turn down sex it probably has nothing to do with you."[9]

Myth 2: Men Are Always in a Hurry

There are two common analogies associated with the myth that men always get turned on very quickly. One is that men are like microwaves—they "heat up" almost instantly—while women are more like slow cookers, in that they slowly simmer and need time to get warmed up.

The other analogy is that of a light switch. For men, this thinking goes, activating sexual desire is as simple and as rapid as the simple flip of a switch, whereas women are slower to engage, like a sliding dimmer switch.

But what if these scenarios are flipped? What if the woman in a marriage is the microwave or the light switch? What if neither spouse is "turned on" every time but instead both vary in their desire depending on the shifting seasons of life or the circumstances they find themselves in?

I once heard a pastor tell the story of a friend who said he loved to cuddle with his wife on the couch and hold hands—and that this activity alone could satisfy him. The pastor said, "I had to step back for a moment and ask, 'Nothing more?'" The underlying message from the pastor was "What's wrong with you? Aren't you a 'real' man? You're supposed to have a sex drive that takes you directly into the bedroom."

I've also heard many times the notion that men prefer to forgo foreplay and get right to intercourse. If you give them an inch, they take a mile, right? If your husband comes up behind you while you're washing dishes and rubs your shoulders, then that's the fast track to intercourse.

Sure, some men might experience this sort of instant revving, but many others require—or even prefer—a slow warm-up.

Myth 3: Men Should Always Be the Initiators

I'm not picking on pastors, I promise, but I do get concerned when someone stands at a podium—many times holding a Bible—and proclaims certain spiritual messages that simply aren't true. Or biblical. This is one of them: that men should be the initiators in the sexual relationship. I've heard countless Christian speakers insist that men should—*should*—pursue and conquer, because that's how God made them.

But when we as women accept and believe this, and then when our husbands don't pursue us as we've been told they're supposed to, it's only natural to become disheartened. We end up not having sex because we sit back and wait . . . and wait . . . and wait. Then we either lose interest or, in our frustration, start blaming the man because we're upset that we waited while he refused to get with the program.

Sure, men can be initiators. But so can women. And that's a good thing. Just ask the Shulammite woman, Solomon's wife in Song of Solomon. She did her share of pursuing her lover (see Song of Solomon 8:1-2).

Myth 4: Sex Should Be Frequent

"What's wrong with my marriage?" Jennifer asked me. "We aren't having sex like normal couples."

"Which normal couples are you referring to?" I said.

"You know . . . other couples," she replied. "My best friend and her husband have sex four times a week. My husband and I have sex barely three times a *month*."

"Do you want to have sex four times a week?"

Jennifer scoffed. "Are you kidding? We don't have that kind

of time! But that's not the point. We *should* be having it that frequently. I think something is wrong with us."

Comparisons. They're so much fun, aren't they?

Actually, comparisons can be incredibly damaging. Let's consider a few examples.

First, Jennifer's friend may or may not be having sex four times a week. If that couple has children living at home, trust me, they likely *aren't* having sex that often. They may be dreaming about that sort of frequency, but they almost certainly don't have that much privacy. Wives in general tend to worry about children catching them in the act, and plenty of husbands do too.

Second, comparisons rarely put you on the "winning" side of the equation—there's always someone doing something more or better than you.

Third (and most important), who decides what is "normal" for you in your bedroom? Normal should never come with a comparison chart. If you're having sex once a week or once a month— or even once every six months— and you and your spouse are content with that amount, then that's your normal, no matter what your best friend and her husband are supposedly doing.

> To be yourself in a world that is constantly trying to make you something else is the greatest accomplishment.
>
> AUTHOR UNKNOWN[10]

I've seen many couples unnecessarily frustrated and discouraged because they compared themselves and their sex lives with what they think is typical or normal.

Once a week can be normal. Once every other week can be normal. Three times a week can be normal. Daily can be normal. But why are we trying to achieve someone else's ideal of "normal"?

More important than achieving some arbitrary frequency

standard is making time for each other and actively loving your spouse as described in 1 Corinthians 13:4-7: "Love is patient and kind; love does not envy or boast; it is not arrogant or rude. It does not insist on its own way; it is not irritable or resentful; it does not rejoice at wrongdoing, but rejoices with the truth. Love bears all things, believes all things, hopes all things, endures all things."

Myth 5: Sex Is for My Pleasure and Release

Yes, sex can provide an intensely pleasurable release. But what happens when it doesn't? Does that mean the sex isn't good? Physical release is just one aspect of the beautiful gift God has given to couples. Sex is also about connection and intimacy—with or without an orgasm. When we make it all about *our* pleasure and *our* release, we run the risk of making sex little more than a means to an end—to use the person we love as a means to get what we want.

That certainly isn't God's design for us in a sexual relationship. Think of sex in marriage as a gift. Husband and wife love each other. We pleasure each other. We enjoy each other. And, if sex is truly a gift, then we gift each other. If an orgasm results, that's great. If it doesn't, sex can still serve its intended purpose of connection, love, intimacy, touch, and, yes, service.

Myth 6: I Need a "Manly Man" Pursuing Me

What's your perception of a "manly man"? Who in the Bible would you say fits that category?

When I ask women this question, the most common answer is David.

That makes sense. After all, consider what one of King Saul's servants said of David: "I have seen a son of Jesse the Bethlehemite who is a skillful musician, a valiant mighty man, a warrior, skillful in speech, and a handsome man; and the Lord is with him" (1 Samuel 16:18, NASB). He sounds like the ideal man, doesn't he?

David was a warrior. He triumphed over the mighty Goliath. And before he spared the Israelites from the wrath of that Philistine giant, David killed both bears and lions to keep them from dining on the sheep he guarded (see 1 Samuel 17:34-37). This mighty man of valor was said to have killed tens of thousands. He became a high-ranking commander in Saul's army, succeeding in many missions against Israel's enemies (see 1 Samuel 18:5-7).

David eventually became king of Israel, and he was beloved of his people. If we measure a man's worth by his success, then David certainly had that going for him.

Yet David was also a broken man. Let's talk about sex here. If we're going to be brutally honest, this king saw another man's wife, lusted after her, then had her brought to his palace (see 2 Samuel 11:2-5). David had no problem violating Bathsheba's sacred marital vow in order to sleep with her. In "David the Man," biblical scholar David Clines describes the account in a stark light: "Even in the Bathsheba episode, the sex is essentially an expression of royal power, and it is much more like rape than love."[11]

To make matters worse, David tried to cover up the infidelity by assigning Bathsheba's husband, Uriah, to the front lines of battle, where the fighting was fiercest. The Bible makes it clear in 2 Samuel 11:14-17 that David was directly responsible for Uriah's death.

Did David later repent? Yes. And he did have a heart for God. Yet we get into dangerous territory when we swoon over this "man's man" without acknowledging the broken humanity he exhibited.

Let's look at it another way: When you take a closer look, do you really want your husband to model his behavior after David's?

How we visually and emotionally perceive the ideal godly husband today is often skewed by the belief that a man actually *can* somehow fulfill all our wishes, desires, and needs—and without us needing to utter a word! Not only can such a man essentially read our minds, he is also an amazing prayer warrior and leader.

Unfortunately, adopting this perspective sets your real-world husband up for failure rather than success.

You don't want your husband to emulate David's many flaws, but instead to choose a very different and far healthier path.

TAKING ON THE LIES AND ASSUMPTIONS

I encourage you to question and evaluate these narratives you've been taught or told, because many of these misconceptions are rampant in our culture and in the church—and, perhaps, even in your own mind. If you've accepted these myths—that men are always ready and willing to have sex, that men are always in a hurry, that men should be the initiators, that normal couples have sex four times a week (or whatever frequency you've heard), that sex is all about release, and that your husband should be a manly man like King David—then it's time to explore a different path. This path might go against what you've heard in the past, but that doesn't somehow make your marriage sexually dysfunctional or less normal. In fact, there's a good chance that reconsidering these misconceptions will help make your marriage *less* dysfunctional.

You and your spouse are the ones who determine what's normal for you. You are not abnormal if you initiate sex with your husband, and your husband is not abnormal if he isn't always ready and willing. If you find that your dissatisfaction with your sex life stems from comparing your relationship with others and with what you've been told, I encourage you to free your mind of these myths and focus instead on the gift of your husband and the sex life that God offers to the two of you.

Every couple is different. Every couple's "normal" is unique to them.

Having said that, you might be dissatisfied for completely legitimate reasons. In your case, perhaps it's not that he is unwilling to have regular or even occasional sex, it's that he's unwilling or unable to have *any* sex, period. You might be in a sexless marriage—what has more recently been described as a "dead bedroom" marriage. If that's where you find yourself, then working toward a solution is about more than just confronting myths and assumptions. It's about getting to the bottom of the problem and finding the real culprit.

And that's what we'll explore next.

PART TWO

The Real Culprits

5

He's Dealing with Physical, Mental, or Neurodiversity Issues

MENTAL OR PHYSICAL HEALTH ISSUES can cause more than emotional distress; they can lead to sexual consequences that many spouses are unaware of. No manner of platitudes, such as "Just relax and it will happen" or "Things will eventually get better," can ease the distress of a wife who feels undesired or unloved. Just as women might lack sexual desire when they're dealing with emotional or physical health issues, so can men.

While women are often more willing to talk about or seek treatment for their health issues, research reveals that many men are not as comfortable getting help—or they don't recognize what's going on, so they don't do anything. Sometimes the result of this inaction is that their sex life, or even their interest in sex, wanes or disappears completely. Their wives, meanwhile, are left to wonder what went wrong. Sometimes they end up making harsh-sounding statements like "What's wrong? This isn't like you" or "Are you taking care of yourself without me again?"

In 2020, the American Psychological Association labeled stress as a "national mental health crisis," one that can cause both emotional and physical changes.[1] Unfortunately, terms like *busy* and *stressed out* are sometimes worn as a badge of honor. What they really mean is that we're living in survival mode. A telltale indicator of a husband's lack of well-being are the words *I'm stressed*, often accompanied by deep, heavy sighs and increasing irritability. Ongoing stress does not bode well for anyone's physical, mental, or sexual health.

PHYSICAL CAUSES OF DESIRE FLUCTUATION

Before jumping to conclusions and Google-diagnosing your husband with some severe psychological disorder that's *maybe* causing a decline in his sex drive, first consider any underlying physical causes. Potential physical causes might include vitamin deficiencies, low testosterone levels, thyroid dysfunction, unhealthy blood pressure or cholesterol numbers, sleep apnea, diabetes, or cardiovascular disease. Sensitivities or allergies associated with chemicals found in fragrances, dyes, and certain foods can also contribute to a loss of energy and libido.[2] Other factors might involve smoking and drug or alcohol use.[3] And, as mentioned earlier, testosterone levels generally decrease over time. In other words, stress is only one contributing factor among many.

Consider taking on the potentially difficult task of encouraging—and perhaps persuading—your husband to make an appointment that could easily rule out or confirm several physical causes. It could be an appointment that helps both of you feel better.

A DOCTOR APPOINTMENT VS. A ROOT CANAL

Perhaps you're already well aware of this, but persuading your husband to see a doctor to discuss issues he would rather ignore can be a difficult undertaking. Imagine how you might steer the conversation:

First, consider framing it as a question of curiosity: "Honey, I'm wondering if the stress you've been dealing with has you worn down?"

If he responds with a growl, sneer, or eye roll, you just might have your answer.

Second, maybe follow up with "Would it be okay if I schedule a doctor appointment for you (and maybe go with you)? I think we'd both love to see you feeling better."

Third, keep in mind that a dismissive response of "I'm fine" is often an indication that he is *not* fine.

Resistance is not uncommon, especially when it comes to making the appointment. While most women would simply schedule their own doctor appointment, husbands can sometimes use a bit of encouragement and support from their wives when it comes to taking care of themselves. I'm not suggesting that you pester your husband or take complete responsibility for his health, but I am encouraging your desire to seek hope and answers for your marriage—not to mention that you are standing alongside him as an advocate and helper.

In my experience, I encounter few men who eagerly advocate for their own physical and emotional health. As much as your husband might resist, consulting a medical professional is a vital part of uncovering any potential health issues. (See the Resources section at the end of this book for more information.)

A first appointment might include a regular physical and routine blood work. Ask for testosterone and thyroid levels to be included in the test. Symptoms of low testosterone might include fatigue, mood swings, depression, decreased sex drive, or erectile dysfunction.[4] Some of these same symptoms, in addition to muscle aches and increased blood cholesterol, can indicate an underactive thyroid (hypothyroidism).[5] Not only is a complete health history important, but so is a discussion with the doctor of the patient's sexual history.

If your husband's health checks out from a physical standpoint, then it's time to consider potential mental health concerns, such as depression or anxiety. Learn what you can about the physician's expertise in mental health care and whether he or she makes referrals to counselors or other therapists (psychiatrists, psychologists) for further diagnostic evaluation.

MENTAL HEALTH ISSUES

When it comes to mental health care, simply obtaining an appointment with an experienced professional these days can require a lot of patience. Seeing the right person is critical, because—depending on where you live—only certain individuals (a general practitioner, a functional medicine doctor, a psychiatrist, or sometimes a physician's assistant) are allowed to prescribe medications. It's important to consult your specific state guidelines. (If you need to speak to a qualified Christian counselor, or want to find one in your area, please contact Focus on the Family at **FocusOnTheFamily.com /GetHelp**. Also refer to the Resources section at the end of this book if you'd like further information on symptoms of depression.)

It's important to treat these symptoms like a "check engine" light on your car's dashboard. (This analogy is especially effective for those husbands who like to handle their own car maintenance.) Stress can and often does mask depression or anxiety symptoms. As wives, it's imperative to understand that anxiety and depression often show up differently in our husbands than it does in us.

ALEJANDRO'S STORY

> In my culture, you go to family for everything and there is not a great deal of trust in doctors or psychiatrists. I was worried about being perceived as weak by my wife and family, but I felt drained all the time. My wife was wonderful and loving and said she would go with me to see the doctor. To be truthful, I had not been to a doctor in more than ten years and the last time was just for stitches. We learned a lot together. I wasn't taking care of myself, but I'm feeling much better now and we're getting some help for our marriage, too.

Keep in mind that anxiety can coexist alongside depression. That's why mental health screenings and diagnostics are so important— they can provide clarity regarding additional treatment options to explore. For example, there are multiple types of anxiety disorders to discuss and navigate with a mental health professional.

ASK ABOUT SIDE EFFECTS

Let's say your husband *is* diagnosed with a mental or physical health issue. If a prescription is part of the treatment, there is a critical question to ask the physician:

What are the sexual side effects of this medication?

Many medications can affect an individual's sex drive, and a competent and compassionate physician should never dismiss this question. And the questions shouldn't end there.

Educate yourselves about your husband's treatment. Don't

hesitate to ask your doctor the embarrassing questions. If you notice a decrease in your husband's sexual desire, bring it up. Challenge those old assumptions—don't assume it's you, and don't assume it's him. Consider attending medical appointments *with* your husband in a supportive capacity. You are a second set of eyes and ears. If your spouse is reluctant, use the "two is better than one" approach. If he is at a physical or emotional low point, at least one of you needs to be clearheaded enough to ask the hard questions that have the potential to change the direction of your sexual relationship.

William Cole, a functional medicine practitioner, states in an article: "Most people don't openly address low libido with their doctors until they're asked some very personal questions and the naked truth is revealed."[6] Cole points out that millions of women (and men) go months or even years without having a healthy, intimate relationship with their spouses—many times because they simply don't bother asking why the problem exists in the first place.

No matter whether a man's desire has diminished slowly or dropped off drastically, there are many factors to consider. Balancing all the possible approaches and treatments is daunting, because while numerous medications might help your husband feel better physically, they also might decrease or eliminate his libido. Also consider that any lab tests might also reflect hidden drug use or excess alcohol consumption.

Do whatever you can to love and support your husband as he learns to better understand the inner workings of his body. While some women have female family members and friends with whom they can discuss female health issues, most men tell me they would rather have a root canal than talk with their buddies about such matters. For one thing, they're concerned that sharing too much personal information sends a message of diminished strength, vitality, and virility.

After all, few men want to appear weak in front of their peers.

THE ADVENTURES OF A NEURODIVERSE MARRIAGE

The term *neurodiversity* refers to the idea that several neurobiological disorders are in fact common variations in the brain, thus you or your spouse might experience one or more of these conditions and bring them to the marriage. An estimated 15–40 percent of the population deals with neurodiversity, and the associated disorders include attention-deficit/hyperactivity disorder (ADHD), autism spectrum disorder (ASD), sensory processing disorder, Tourette's syndrome, dyslexia, dyspraxia, and other neurobiological conditions that occur during gestational development.[7] (I've included this information to increase awareness that many of these mental health and physical health concerns are quite common and can also appear concurrently. Various patterns of behavior and emotions tie into the neurodivergent population, which would take a whole book and then some to fully address!)

Let me acknowledge the obvious: I will likely disappoint numerous wives by not addressing the specific condition(s) that you or your husband might have and how they might affect your sex life. The disorder I'm most familiar with on a personal and professional level is ADHD, and I will share some of my own marital story regarding this disorder later in the book.

If you are a neurodivergent spouse, or are married to one, please educate yourself on the various adventures that neurodiversity adds to a marriage. For example, if ADHD is present in your marriage, almost anything by marriage consultant Melissa Orlov is worth reading. Orlov is the author of *The ADHD Effect on*

Marriage and *The Couple's Guide to Thriving with ADHD*. Another helpful resource is clinical psychologist Russell A. Barkley's book *When an Adult You Love Has ADHD*.

One primary concern I hear expressed by wives of husbands with ADHD is the significant amount of mind-wandering they observe during sexual encounters with their husbands. There are also ADHD-related challenges involving an awareness of a partner's sexual needs and the inability to recall specific likes and dislikes based on previous encounters. It's easy to be upset by a husband's inattentiveness, but many times the disorder itself is to blame. In some situations, ADHD can also lead to impulsivity, hyperfocus, and hypersexuality—better known as compulsive sexual behavior or sex addiction.

The most important thing I've learned in my own marriage to an amazing husband with ADHD is that his brain functions in different, brilliant, astounding, and unique ways. He is, in all honesty, quite mischievous and quirky at times. My husband works hard at serving and loving me well in the ways that God calls him to. It doesn't come easily to him, but he makes a concerted effort. He's not without moments of forgetfulness, but he demonstrates heartfelt remorse when he does forget.

I've learned to separate the man I love from the disorder. After all, the person and the condition are often very different.

How so?

If your husband had cancer or multiple sclerosis—disorders of the body—you would understand that they are only a minuscule part of who he is and how God designed him. The same mindset applies when you are married to a neurodivergent spouse: Refusing to blame your husband for something he can't control opens the door to greater empathy and compassion. Try to approach the neurodiverse aspects of your marriage with love and humor. (That's what this wife tries to do with her ADHD husband!)

One weekend morning, while doing chores around the house, my husband and I casually discussed making pizza for dinner. Later that afternoon, as we spent some time cuddling and kissing in bed, my husband unexpectedly asked, "Do we have mushrooms for the pizza?" I was speechless for a moment, fully naked, then smiled widely and cracked up. Unfortunately, my response immediately diminished his physical enthusiasm. My husband didn't catch on to what was so funny, and he thought I was laughing at him. I immediately hugged him, which brought about a positive shift in mood. Instead of feeling anger and frustration toward him for choosing to think about mushrooms instead of my body, I chose love and humor. So now when I want to connect with him physically, I'll ask, "Got mushrooms?" This lighthearted question essentially means, "Are you interested?" My husband has welcomed this phrase enthusiastically.

The neurodivergent individual is often highly skilled and excels in many areas of life due to his or her ability to hyperfocus. Activities that are fun and pleasurable usually receive that focus, and one would assume that sex would qualify as one of those enjoyable activities. However, couples in which a partner is neurodivergent often describe the exact opposite. When it comes to sex and neurodiversity, the struggle is very real.

Many wives whose husbands have been diagnosed with ADHD still struggle to understand the sexual challenges of neurodiversity. They sometimes make sweeping declarations like "If he really loved me and cared, he would remember what is important. He would be able to focus and remember how my body responds."

I ask these women to consider believing that he does try—that he really tries—rather than assuming the worst. Here's the challenge: If this is your situation, extend a moment of grace and patience, along with a lighthearted smile, and say, "Over here, honey—this is the spot I love."

How might a subtle change in your heart, words, and smile shift the mood in your relationship? One small shift might pull him back toward you, emotionally and physically. Compassion extended outward often results in more compassion and understanding boomeranging back to you. And that outcome is a win for both of you.

COMPASSION REGARDING MENTAL HEALTH CARE

Sometimes I hear from Christians struggling with mental health issues whose well-meaning friends and family urge, "Be patient. God will provide healing. Why would you want to take medications?" This is just another ill-advised way to heap on the shame and doubt that someone struggling with mental health might already feel. We need to do better as a faith community.

Believers need to be like a sign that reads: "We Have a NO SHAME Policy!"

God absolutely has the power to heal ailments, and prayer is essential. But two more elements are necessary—compassion and grace. Perfect physical, spiritual, and emotional health don't exist in a fallen world. Rather than shame or judge our brothers and sisters in Christ for using medications and seeking mental health treatment, why not love them and support them through the process? Besides, showing compassion and grace for their suffering is far more likely to promote healing than guilt or shame.

I'll leave the rest of the preaching on this particular topic to the pastors who support and advocate for mental health care. I do, however, want to address another touchy subject before we move on.

Most of the men I work with in ministry or in my counseling office are reluctant to share their concerns about mental health issues until they are at a point of desperation. They deal with tremendous fear that someone might notice their issues and perceive them as lacking in strength or vitality. Writing in the *Washington Post*, University of Southern California professor and men's mental health advocate Joseph Harper explained, "I have watched mothers and wives literally drag the men they love into my office. I often struggle with some male patients to pull information about their emotional issues out of them because they are so reluctant to speak. Others simply downplay their problems saying things like, 'It's not really a big deal,' or 'My wife is blowing this out of proportion.'"[8]

If you are wife to a husband who is reluctant to seek help—for a mental health issue or any other problems—please carefully consider the following:

- Honest, frank, and loving talk needs to happen together as a couple.
- Carefully and prayerfully examine what you believe your needs are.
- There are no quick or easy solutions to reigniting his sexual desire.

We can never go wrong with compassion, kindness, and patience when someone we love is struggling, either physically or mentally. After all, don't we long for the same empathy? Love instead of judgment will touch the hearts of those we love just about every time.

He's Meeting His Needs Elsewhere

IN THIS BOOK'S OPENING CHAPTERS, we learned that many familiar narratives or societal messages presented as truth are not actually valid. For example, consider closely the following outlandish statement:

All men look at porn and masturbate, right? Guys need a release. Why should my husband be any different?

Consider who promotes this message and how it's presented as infallible—which makes it feel like brainwashing. The porn industry, for example, constantly reinforces this idea, which then infiltrates our homes as it gets passed from father to son, husband to wife, mother to daughter, friend to friend, and church member to church member. Anytime I challenge the lie, I receive a shoulder shrug and a resigned admission: "That's just the way it is. I have to accept it as a woman if I want a man in my life."

But this is just one more narrative that seeks to demolish the intimacy that God intends for couples to experience in a healthy Christian marriage. *Knowing* each other deeply, both inside and outside the bedroom, is crucial for developing emotional, spiritual, and physical intimacy.

Yet deception, dysfunction, and distortion related to God-designed intimacy have their roots intertwined in the hearts and minds of young boys increasingly early. Multiple studies indicate that the average age of first exposure to pornography is between eleven and twelve years old.[1] According to Covenant Eyes, an organization that provides porn-filtering and accountability software, "Today's graphic online pornography commandeers the brain's neurology with what science calls super-normal stimuli. In basic scientific terms, super-normal stimuli are artificially enhanced. They subvert and hijack our natural appetites and motivational systems and overstimulate our neural pathways."[2]

By the time most men start dating, their neural pathways have been overwhelmed with artificially enhanced lust and fantasy. No wonder so many husbands today struggle with real-world intimacy when their primary means of female contact has been with pornographic images and their primary physical pleasure has occurred through masturbation. However pleasurable this behavior might seem to a man, exposure to pornography can lead to negative emotions such as excessive stress, anger, anxiety and tension, loneliness or rejection, low self-esteem, a sense of failure, and fatigue.[3] Yet many current and future wives fail to understand the consequences of porn exposure.

SANDRA'S STORY

My husband and I met in 2011 at church and married in 2015. We were deeply affectionate while dating, and

I thought we were the perfect couple. We were a little bit older than most newlyweds, but we still waited to be intimate on our wedding night. What I thought would be a wonderful honeymoon was very discouraging; we only made love once in seven days, and my husband kept saying he was exhausted. He would cuddle, kiss, and hold me, but he had trouble maintaining an erection. And that usually caused him to give up.

One afternoon during our honeymoon, while we were sitting on the beach together, his phone buzzed. I looked over, and what appeared on the screen stunned me. He was looking for someone to give him a lap dance at a local strip club while I watched. Within a few short months, our sex life quickly diminished as he was constantly viewing porn. He finally revealed that he had been into porn since middle school and had started visiting strip clubs as soon as he was old enough to get in.

I've long struggled to understand why he lied to me for four years while we dated, why he has a lack of interest in genuine intimacy, and what feels like laziness in his attitude toward working on mutual pleasure. I'm not interested in watching porn with him and feel deeply betrayed. I've brought up marriage counseling numerous times, but all I receive in reply is a shoulder shrug.

A recent *Psychology Today* article titled "The Sexual Secrets Men and Women Hide from Their Partners" noted a study of college students that found the most common secret men conceal is pornography use. (Among women, this same secret was number four on the list.)[4]

A distorted mindset dares to suggest, "I prefer to view porn because my future spouse may never fulfill my needs," or "I'll never find a spouse if I reveal my secrets."

So what happens when a man with this distorted mindset marries an unsuspecting wife with a healthy desire for sex? She is a willing participant, but she is not honored, respected, or held in high regard. Instead she receives indifference, humiliation, or perhaps coercion to perform unsavory acts tied to what her husband has seen online. A husband's porn consumption tends to magnify every emotional, physical, and spiritual insecurity a woman has about herself. It likewise invalidates her beauty and worth. Yet all too often we brush off this behavior as "something all men do."

Husbands frequently respond with some version of the following statement when I bring up porn use: "It's what I *need* to release and de-stress." They have little or no understanding about how porn distorts perceptions of godly intimacy in marriage.

When I'm doing premarital counseling with seriously dating or engaged couples, I schedule one private session with each member of the couple. I frequently ask the men, "I'm curious about potential porn use in your life. How young were you when you were first introduced to it? How often might you find yourself craving access to porn and masturbation?"

They usually stare at me, dumbfounded that I'm somehow aware of their secret. I then ask, "Have you shared this secret with your girlfriend/fiancée?"

Whether or not the man is a Christian, I am typically met with the following replies:

- It's no big deal.
- It enhances my sexuality.
- People are prudes if they don't like it.
- It makes sex more exciting.
- Every man needs it.
- Why would I tell her? She might leave me.

My contention is that porn is destructive to marriages and eradicates the development of healthy sexuality. How do I know this? I encounter the negative effects of pornography almost daily in my work as a counselor. I've learned that many wives feel trapped in their marriages and have become resigned to accepting what is known as a pornographic style of relating with their husbands. Let's look at what that means.

PORN DEMOLISHES HEALTHY INTIMACY

Andrew J. Bauman, cofounder and director of the Christian Counseling Center (CCC), describes a pornographic style of relating (PSR) in marriage—a style of relating "learned when pornography becomes your primary teacher or guide in your sexual development."[5] Most husbands don't realize how porn usage distorts perceptions of healthy intimacy in marriage. In addition, they can and do lie about their chronic porn use.

Women who don't know the truth about a partner's porn use might (often unknowingly) choose a sexually unhealthy man to marry, not because they've deceived themselves but because *they have been deceived and lied to*. With prolonged porn use, the unhealthy sexual behaviors listed in the chart on the next page will emerge. These unhealthy behaviors are typically connected to a pornographic style of relating. For example, a PSR mindset *objectifies* women, while a sexually healthy individual *honors* them. PSR ultimately dishonors a spouse.

However, when porn is nonexistent in someone's life, the sexually healthy behaviors listed in the chart are more evident, thus honoring the spouse and the marriage. In Bauman's book *The Sexually Healthy Man: Essays on Spirituality, Sexuality and Restoration*, the author provides some characteristics of sexuality in marriage that help provide a greater understanding of unhealthy versus healthy sexuality:

UNHEALTHY	vs.	HEALTHY
Emotionally Distant	vs.	Emotionally Present
Secrets/Hidden Life	vs.	Authentic/True
Isolation	vs.	Community
Fantasy	vs.	Reality
Arrogance	vs.	Humility
Immature	vs.	Mature
Objectify	vs.	Honor
Selfish	vs.	Mutual
Aggression	vs.	Kindness
Demanding	vs.	Patient
Insecurity	vs.	Strength
Ashamed	vs.	Unashamed[6]

Recognizing the common outcomes of porn use means that you no longer ignore those "Why does he do this?" or "Why does he act that way?" questions when you approach your husband about sex and desire. You understand that there is a reason he feels that he can't be honest about his struggles—not only shame, but often a deep-seated fear you might leave him. This realization could be the beginning of a profoundly uncomfortable and vulnerable conversation—one that hopefully leads to finding help for him, for you, and for your marriage.

In that moment, I want to caution you: It can be difficult to convey a message of "It's time for a change" and "I'm no longer okay with where we're at" while remaining calm. Yet it's critical. Becoming intensely emotional or issuing ultimatums will *never* make a husband feel like you're approachable and safe to share with. Do your best to speak truthfully and lovingly regarding what needs to change for you to feel sexually secure with him and regarding what honors you and your marriage. If he feels shamed, blamed, or attacked, his walls will remain up and he'll continue to hide.

Two Christian organizations that offer help to couples facing this issue are Pure Desire Ministries (PureDesire.org) and Naked Truth Project (NakedTruthProject.com), both of which have been at the forefront of helping Christians break the cycle of porn addiction with support groups for more than twenty years.

In *Restoring What's Been Lost: Six Steps to Claiming Victory over Porn Addiction*, an e-book offered through Marriagetrac.com, I address additional steps a wife can take with her husband toward whole and healthy intimacy, such as learning how to know when he's genuinely repentant and when he's not, and how to know when he's working to remain clean and rebuild trust.

I implore you to no longer accept excuses, counter-blaming, defensiveness, justification, or resistance to seeking help for your marriage. It's time to open your eyes to the issues in his heart, your home, and your marriage. These are the words you need to hear from him: "Yes, let's get the help we need. I'll do whatever it takes."

As my husband, Jim, and I wrote in *Restoring What's Been Lost*:

> If you are to heal as a couple, you cannot remain isolated and hide in the four walls of your home. We understand, it's horribly embarrassing to let anyone know the battle your marriage is up against. This is why sharing with a trusted Christian friend, small group leader, or pastor is essential. Their prayers for your marriage and for you individually provide a layer of protection for the healing journey ahead.[7]

From the very beginning of this process, you'll want to feel supported, loved, and encouraged to seek professional assistance. You'll want wise counsel and a safe place to share your burdens. A good first step is finding counselors and support groups skilled in porn-addiction or sex-addiction recovery. Christian resources are available to target your specific needs. (Calling Focus on the Family at 855-771-HELP or visiting **FocusOnTheFamily.com/Pornography** is a great first step in learning about available Christian resources and assistance.) What's more, I'll share additional information in the Resources section at the end of this book. I want you to be as informed as possible and to get the help your marriage needs.

Just take that first step toward healing; there will be more steps to follow.

NO MORE SILENCE

Every week I see marriages with significant desire differences. While there are numerous reasons for this dilemma, I've witnessed compulsive sexual behaviors increasing at alarming rates and damaging countless marriages. When wives stay silent because they fear confrontation, they send a message that they quietly accept their husbands' lack of desire or effort, their anger, or their withdrawal. It's like opening your door and inviting hundreds of highly infectious people into your home. In much the same way, you are allowing a virus to infect your marriage. As psychologist and author Henry Cloud emphasizes in his book *Boundaries in Marriage*, "You get what you tolerate."[8]

Maybe your husband has been rejecting you for months or even years. In those circumstances, the two questions I'm asked more than any others are "Is there hope?" and "What do I do if he refuses to seek help?"

Absolutely there is hope, but that comes with moving past your worries and no longer tolerating what's been tossed into your lap. It's time to seek the professional help and healing you so desperately need for yourself—whether or not your husband seeks counseling on his own. (Seeking professional help will also help you process your pain and work through tough decisions regarding your future.)

> A victorious life is not stumbled upon; it's cultivated. It's the result of being bold, brave—*fearless*—when everything in you wants to cower in defeat.
>
> TRACEY MITCHELL[9]

The various questions about what to do next are why Jim and I wrote *Restoring What's Been Lost*. We wanted to offer guidance with the following steps:

- Moving forward with courage
- Watching, listening, and praying
- Becoming an agent of positive change
- Choosing community and connection
- Seeking professional help
- Being patient for the results[10]

What moves you and your husband down the path toward healthy sexuality is no longer tolerating what's infiltrated your marriage. When we fail to talk about porn usage meaningfully, the associated lust remains hidden and seductive. I want to state this very clearly: *You* are not responsible for keeping him away from porn. That's *his* job.

THE OSTRICH SYNDROME

The reluctance of many to address the problem of pornography is similar to sticking our heads in the sand like an ostrich, pretending that the battle around us does not exist. The increasing rate of porn use speaks to our lack of recognition about the detrimental effects of pornography on our youth, families, and marriages. As of November 2022, the top three porn sites in the world reported 22.64 billion visitors a month, or more than 270 billion visitors a year![11]

Even as many Christians sound the alarm, the overall silence is still deafening. We are reaping what we've been tolerating, which sends a subtle but deadly message of acceptance regarding porn's emotional destruction and spiritual depletion.

Sit with that reality a moment.

The damage that porn causes is staggering because it desensitizes a user's mind and body. Porn is not a harmless hobby or a "stress reliever." In 2016, the Barna Group published a study called *The Porn Phenomenon*, reporting that "one in five youth pastors (21 percent) and one in seven senior pastors (14 percent) admitted they currently use porn." The study also reported that 40 percent of practicing Christians who actively seek out porn feel comfortable with how much porn they use, and only one-third of practicing Christian porn users say they feel a sense of guilt when they use porn."[12]

This might help explain why many Christian men and women hesitate to go to their churches for help with their heartbreak and pain. Yet we desperately need community in our search for healing. Women do not need to hear that their husbands' sinful choices are somehow *their* issue. This only perpetuates unhealthy notions about sexuality, and it fails to model healthy Christian marriage for our children and for future generations.

A PASTOR'S WIFE'S STORY

I wear a fake smile every Sunday as he preaches in front of the church. Only I know what he's looked at all week. Only I know that he's not touched me in years. My heart is broken, because the moment I say anything to him

about my concerns and our need to get help, that's when
the floodgates of anger open. This is a huge secret that
I cannot share with anyone. I don't know what is going
to happen to our ministry, to our children, or to our
marriage. My boys are at the age when they have questions
about sex, and there is no way I want my husband
speaking to them. I want my sons to respect women.

This woman's pain is palpable. Her story helps explain why so
many women remain silent about their circumstances and hide
their husbands' struggles with pornography—never revealing the
sin or pursuing the help they so desperately want.

This wife's story also points to concerns about young men—in
this case, her sons—growing up in a porn-saturated culture. The
goal of the nonprofit organization Culture Reframed is to help
build resilience and resistance in young people to hypersexualized
media and pornography. Founder and president Gail Dines is also
the author of *Pornland: How Porn Has Hijacked Our Sexuality.*
Writing about Dines's efforts in *Psychology Today,* author and anti-
trafficking advocate Mitzi Perdue explains, "As Dines sees it, pornography has become the world's de facto system of sex education.
It's surprising how pervasive this system is." Perdue concludes:
"It's a public health crisis. A generation of young people are being
raised who don't understand love and mutuality and empathy. It's
critical to do better. It's critical to act."[13]

Action is essential in establishing a spiritual culture that asks
hard questions of ourselves and our brothers and sisters in Christ.
Not the easy, comfortable stuff, but penetrating questions about
our individual and marital struggles. Questions that dig beneath
the surface and require an authentic response other than *fine* or
good. Questions that no longer allow us to keep sticking our heads
in the sand.

7

He Struggles with Insecurities Too

WOMEN AREN'T THE ONLY ONES who hear and embrace messages from the church, the culture, friends, and family. Men do as well. They pick up on their perceived inadequacies and often feel as if they are less than men. They've heard that they are expected to *just know* what a woman needs and wants at all times, as though it's a skill as instinctive as breathing.

Trouble is, mind reading is not instinctive. It simply doesn't exist.

Moreover, men try to develop soft, emotionally sensitive spots in their hearts and minds while still remaining thoroughly masculine. And if a man perceives a message from his wife that he's failed or let her down, his response isn't *Try, try again*, but rather *Never again*.

Women, meanwhile, are often immensely critical of themselves and struggle with comparisons to other women. We know how we feel when our skills and intelligence—whether in the workplace, at home, or as mothers—are questioned. And that doesn't include the impact on our confidence when a husband says, "Honey, that seems like more than a little chocolate treat" or "Do you have something else you could wear?" Let's be candid—a single misguided comment can unleash an emotional tidal wave.

In the same way, have you considered how one seemingly innocuous remark about his shirt being snug, his looking sloppy, or his indulging in one too many hot dogs can diminish his sense of worth and connection to you? *But he's a man, and he will brush it off quickly, right?* But what if he doesn't? What if your husband is not one of those—you know—super-masculine, warrior types? What if he's not a King David kind of guy? What if he really wants to meet your sexual needs but simply lacks confidence? What if he feels deeply inadequate?

THE HUNT FOR A NEW MALE NARRATIVE

One new narrative we can adopt is *He's trying. He's making a genuine effort.* If our mindset is that he continually falls short, we need to step back and observe our husband's words, body language, and signs of dissatisfaction that might indicate his insecurities. We say that we want him to know us deeply and be attuned to our world, but are we adjusting to his?

- Have you ever considered how your husband feels about his own body?
- Does he carry himself with confidence?
- Does the slightest correction about something he's done wrong bring on a flood of irritation or anger?

- Have you considered that he wants to hear you say he is desirable, sexy, or handsome?
- How is he at handling the stressors of caring for you? Your kids? Your home?
- How is he at handling financial stress?
- How is he at handling the care of elderly parents?
- Have you noticed whether he *verbalizes* or *internalizes* his worries?
- Have you noticed differences in his body language when he can't fix something, when he's sharing his struggles, or when he only wants a listening ear?
- Would he feel more secure and connected with you if you noticed him doing things well rather than pointing out something he missed?
- Have you considered that his sexual desire might ebb and flow based on how he feels about himself? He might exude confidence outwardly yet feel inadequate on the inside.
- Do you ever compare your husband with other husbands or other men in your world?

Transparency is vital here. You need to be completely honest with yourself in answering these questions. Seldom do growth and change happen in our lives without transparency and vulnerability.

THE MOST IMPORTANT QUESTION OF THEM ALL

Have you ever, knowingly or unknowingly, sent your husband the message that you think he is inadequate?

In the more than twenty years I've spent working with engaged and married couples, I've noticed that any perceived message of *inadequacy* can create a vacuum that hinders emotional connection and can drain sexual desire out of a man in a nanosecond.

Let's imagine some scenarios. In the first one, you begin to share with your husband a series of concerns about work or a friend. You make it clear that all you want is a listening ear, not someone to help fix the issue. Now watch his body. He might bite his cheek, emit heavy sighs, or sit on his hands—all because he cannot fix it for you. *Yet the moment you allow him to offer a solution and thank him for his insights, he might follow you anywhere!*

In the second scenario, you're going out for a nice romantic dinner and hope this date helps reignite the missing spark of physical connection once you arrive back home. As you're preparing to leave, you request a quick wardrobe adjustment from your husband: "Change those jeans, dear. They look sloppy and make your rear end sag." *Change your delivery to "I love your dark blue jeans because they make your rear look great," then observe how he carries himself with confidence in order to please you!*

In the third scenario, your husband has spent all afternoon mowing the lawn, pulling weeds, trimming bushes, and cleaning the garage. But rather than tell him how great everything looks, you find that one spot he didn't get just right. You might decide to fix it while he's away—but is it really worth it? He'll likely notice that he didn't do the job to your satisfaction, which might end up making things worse. *Instead, simply thank him and then let it go. Besides, one spot won't make the neighbors think your husband is a failure. And perfection is boring anyway!*

His reaction to all three scenarios might be subtle or hard to read, such as a sharp comment spoken under his breath. Or maybe he reacts like he often does when he is tired or has a lot on his mind. At first it's easy to dismiss his reactions, but ongoing messages of inadequacy will inevitably lead to feelings of frustration or resentment, and those feelings can lead to angry outbursts—or the opposite: the silent treatment. Under no circumstances do I condone outbursts of anger or the silent treatment, but I want you to understand what's prompting your husband's behavior when he can't put a name to what he's feeling and experiencing.

HE'S NOT SUPERMAN

Your husband is not a superhero. He doesn't have the physical prowess of Superman, nor is he emotionally bulletproof. Yet many portrayals in the movies, on television, and even on social media depict an unrealistic standard of masculinity regarding how men are *supposed to* look on the outside and feel on the inside. This false picture only adds to the typical man's insecurities, especially when we mistakenly believe he should have no insecurities at all.

What if your husband's physique is, say, distinctly average? He might not admit it, but he's likely just as self-conscious about his body as you are about yours. He might be incredibly thin, somewhat thicker in the middle, or shorter than you, but part of him still wants you to think he's the sexiest man alive. (Depending on his background and influences, he might already feel pressure to know how to use all the tools in the garage, repair the broken railing and hang drywall, plus change the oil in your car. And let's not forget the pressure he feels to be the most caring and sensitive lover—completely in tune with you whenever you have even a tinge of desire for him.)

Compare the expectations your husband faces with society's skewed standards of femininity. Are we perpetuating an unreasonable standard of masculinity? Are we setting our husbands up for failure by failing to see them through God's eyes? Remember that your husband is only human, and he wants a wife beside him to help carry the burdens of life.

When we step in as his helper (see Genesis 2:18), we draw our husband's heart, body, and energy toward us. If you don't do this, he might feel as though it's you against him, and when he perceives that from you, he will often withdraw sexually. It's time to erase from your mind the outline of the perfect sexual man—the guy who causes emotional bullets to bounce off his chest—because that shape is not the image of a loving, godly man.

SOME MODIFICATIONS REQUIRED

I've spent lots of time looking for messages online designed to help hurting marriages. This effort proved particularly challenging after the COVID-19 pandemic began. Instead, I found lots of sermons on anxiety and depression. Those messages were deeply needed, of course, but because so many marriages are struggling post-pandemic, I was looking for something else.

After a great deal of searching, I found a message for marriages that seemed promising, so I asked my husband to listen to it with me. And while the pastor offered solid biblical teaching, his picture of male sexuality left us rather dismayed.

This is the same pastor I described earlier who teased a man who liked to cuddle, then suggested that men have a supernatural ability to make *anything* sexual. Whether men are maintaining the car or doing basic household tasks, the pastor suggested, they are always *ready to go*.

The congregation chuckled, and I'm sure that some of them subscribe to this as normal male behavior. I asked my husband, "Do you think men have a supernatural ability to make anything sexual? Were you aware of this gift?" Imagine being a husband in the congregation who genuinely loves cuddling. Would this man think, *What's wrong with me?* Meanwhile, the hurting wife in the audience who hasn't had sex in months or even years might be thinking, *I'll take one of those "ready-to-go" husbands.*

It is perfectly okay to be a loving, godly man who enjoys a little bit more cuddle and a little less sex. The problem occurs when the husband *only* wants to cuddle and the wife is *hoping* for more. The key word here is *hoping* instead of *verbalizing*. Many women struggle to verbalize their needs, particularly sexual needs. They often share with me, "If my husband were in tune with me, he would *know* my needs." Once again, we run the risk of expecting husbands to add mind reading to their list of superpowers. I've never yet met a husband who is able to "just know."

It doesn't help matters when a husband's thought processes feed into his insecurities and feelings of inadequacy. He begins to question his manliness. Perhaps he begins to think, *She can't possibly love me if . . .*

- *I'm not muscular.*
- *I don't have a 32-inch waist.*
- *I don't have handyman skills.*
- *I'm not pursuing her enough sexually.*
- *I don't know exactly how and when she needs help.*
- *I'm not able to read her desire signals.*
- *I should be a better father.*
- *I should be better at managing the finances.*

Notice the similarities at the beginning of each thought: *I'm not*, *I don't*, and *I should*. These feelings can leave him experiencing shame. Remember that your husband's heart is not capable of deflecting emotional bullets. In fact, it might be more tender than you ever imagined. And when an emotional bullet does pierce his heart, that's when you might notice decreased sexual desire, isolation, impatience, or even anger directed your way. That's what happens when messages of shame or *not good enough* are internalized.

WHEN SELF-ESTEEM PLUMMETS

When attempting to understand insecurities regarding self-esteem, as well as the impact of media on self-image, we first need to recognize that most of the information on this topic has traditionally focused on women. Yet research is emerging that points to male struggles with eating disorders, anabolic steroid use, and body image concerns.[1] More men nowadays are stepping forward to share their pain and struggles.

According to Viren Swami, a professor of social psychology at Anglia Ruskin University, "It's estimated that between 30% and 40% of men are anxious about their weight and that up to 85% are dissatisfied with their muscularity. Many men desire a lean and muscular physique—which is often seen as synonymous with masculinity."[2] Males begin to perceive numerous physical flaws starting in adolescence. These perceptions often carry through to anxieties about intimacy and sexual performance with a wife.

ROBERT'S STORY

I work out daily and still do not see myself as muscular or even handsome. Meanwhile, I have people tell me I should be on the cover of GQ. I'm obsessive about my diet and how I look in everything I wear, but I still struggle to feel confident with my wife when we have sex. Many times, all I'm thinking about is whether she sees any fat around my sides. Stuff like this distracts me and I struggle to keep my mind on her and on us, which means I don't maintain an erection easily.

It only takes a moment of struggle in maintaining an erection—something all men experience at some point—and the promise of future sexual encounters becomes a gamble. One incident can seem catastrophic, raising alarm bells and the anxious thought *I'll never be able to again.*

It's as though one instance of his body's failure to perform becomes a self-fulfilling prophecy for every other time that follows. *If it happened once*, the thinking goes, *it will happen again.* And it's not in just the man's head. The wife might be thinking, *His body rejected me and will always reject me.* In moments of uncertainty, this is where an abundance of grace and patience toward each other can help overcome our feelings of insecurity. Few speak about how this is normal across all ages, from teenagers to men in their eighties. Men don't talk about this issue with their buddies, and wives rarely discuss it with their girlfriends.

Why is this such a taboo topic? After all, nothing in the human body functions optimally 100 percent of the time. Yet our reluctance to discuss it isn't likely to change anytime soon.

We often fail to consider the numerous factors that can affect a man's sexual function, such as how he's feeling about himself physically and emotionally. Does your husband feel safe sharing his insecurities with you? If not, he will hide them. You want him to understand your fears and help meet your needs, but are you offering him the same understanding and support in the areas where he struggles? Areas such as

- how he feels about his body,
- how he feels about his sexual performance, and
- how confident he feels about his ability to please you.

For example, how does he feel about how he appears to other men? Particularly at the gym or in the locker room? (Men make comparisons too.) Consider that his heart is sensitive, fragile, tender, and vulnerable.

Women understand how one small comment about our bodies

can cause us to reel emotionally. Do we fully recognize the impact of one critical comment and how it might affect him?

Do we understand his feelings of pride? Not an unbiblical pride, but pride in his accomplishments and in working hard for us and for the family. Do we understand the joy he experiences when he sees his wife smile with pride at *him*? And how often do we tell him that he's amazing?

Husbands need affirmation too. Let him know that he is your loving, good, and godly husband. Genuinely consider believing that he's trying, really trying. Not perfectly, of course, but he's your husband, not your Savior. We all fall short every day, but that shouldn't keep you from telling him how much you value and appreciate him.

8

He Has Been Victimized

PAST ABUSE—WHETHER IT'S SEXUAL, verbal, spiritual, psychological, or emotional—can follow all of us into the bedroom. This includes men. For example, he might be haunted by an unspoken experience he endured during childhood, to the degree that when a close relationship goes wrong, those memories suddenly wreak havoc during his most vulnerable and intimate moments. That experience is likely something he has never shared with anyone, including his wife, and because she doesn't know this part of his past, she might unintentionally reopen a wound by bringing up a sexual issue in an area that previously brought him pain and shame.

Many wives have never considered the possibility that their husband's innocence was stolen, perhaps at a very young age. Maybe he was groomed by an older child with whom there was a power imbalance, or maybe he was exposed to pornography by a friend or sibling. Maybe it was a seemingly innocent scenario of "Show me yours and I'll show you mine."

Sadly, one-third of such cases are child-on-child abuse with both children under the age of eighteen.[1] The Rape, Abuse, and Incest National Network (RAINN) estimates that two-thirds of victims are ages twelve to seventeen, and one-third are under the age of twelve. Childhood sexual abuse victims are acquainted with or related to their abuser more than 90 percent of the time.[2] And at least one in six males has been sexually abused or assaulted.[3]

If your husband comes from a divorced family, a newly single parent can unknowingly introduce a series of dating partners who first groom and then abuse that parent's children. These abusers include both men and women.

In my experience, women are more likely than men to come forward and share their abuse stories. More recently, however, I'm seeing an increase in males disclosing past sexual abuse. No matter the gender, coming forward takes courage. Male abuse survivors hold on to their secrets because they feel like no one will ever believe them—especially if an older female such as a sister was the aggressor.

I've heard many wives ask, "How would I ever know if this happened to my husband?" I can offer several hints, but no certainties. There is no comprehensive list of the indicators of childhood sexual abuse, but I will present the hints that arise most often in marriage counseling. With that in mind, I caution wives to handle their inquiries cautiously rather than jump to assumptions.

Hint 1: Lack of Emotion

In the aftermath of childhood abuse, one area of concern involves something called *blunt emotional range*, which describes someone who is extremely disconnected from their emotions and finds them almost impossible to express. We refer to this feeling of emptiness or inner apathy as *blunting*. Such a limited range of emotions can cause a sense of restlessness and lead to reduced sexual desire. Many individuals in this state also doubt their ability to accomplish life goals. Depression, which also results in a lack of desire, can be a common denominator with blunting. Many abuse victims and their spouses never make this connection between childhood trauma and a lack of desire later in life.

Hint 2: Strong Emotions and Being Quick to Anger

In some circumstances, the post-traumatic stress disorder (PTSD) that results from past sexual abuse can lead to moments wherein the abuse victim experiences flashbacks. You might notice your husband "spacing out," experiencing forgetfulness, or even describing the feeling of being outside his body. Many men are more prone to display anger and lower stress tolerance than sadness because sadness is often (mistakenly) associated with being vulnerable or weak. Pay attention to whether your husband feels powerless, ashamed, overlooked, anxious, stressed, or triggered, as well as whether anger seems to appear out of nowhere.

Hint 3: Risky Behaviors

Other possible indicators of past abuse are heightened sexuality, porn use, and the use of addictive substances. These signals might seem counterintuitive to what we believe an abuse survivor needs, at least in terms of seeking comfort, but these behaviors are worth mentioning. "Sexually abused boys often become men who have difficulty distinguishing among sex, love, nurturance, affection, and abuse," says Richard Gartner, the founding director of the sexual abuse program at the William Alanson White Institute.[4] Addictive behaviors are quite common among sexual abuse survivors.

Hint 4: Reluctance to Trust

There is a great deal to overcome in working to earn the trust of an abuse victim. Encouraging a man to trust you to the point that he'll reveal his most personal secrets might take years. Seldom do I see men disclose their past abuse prior to marriage for fear that the one person they finally feel close to and safe with will decide to leave them. These men desire love and emotional intimacy, but they can numb out (and quickly lose an erection) during a sexual encounter. Therefore, trusting their wives to comfort and hold them (that cuddling thing we like to do after lovemaking) might be completely off limits depending on how their abusers used touch to lure them into compliance. What a husband who was abused needs is a wife who is empathetic and willing to walk with him throughout the healing process.

Hint 5: Overprotectiveness

Overprotectiveness tends to show up after you and your husband have children. The secret fears within him—that you might know nothing about—can intensify as your children grow closer to the age your husband was at the time of his first abuse experience.

STEVEN'S TRAUMATIC CHILDHOOD

Steven was very cautious about having anyone watch their son, including both sets of grandparents. He was also opposed to any overnight stays. Eventually his wife, Cathryn, started expressing her desire for a multi-night getaway for just the two of them. They also discussed plans for having a second child soon since their little boy was already four years old. Cathryn's frustration was growing because every time she tried to bring up a getaway, she was met with resistance. Whenever Steven expressed his concern about leaving their son for three days, his body language shifted and he became highly agitated. He raised his voice and even started shaking.

Cathryn finally stated what she felt was obvious: "Honey, something about this is so unsettling to you and feels so unbalanced." That was when everything poured out of Steven—how his stepgrandfather had sexually abused him at the age of five. Because their son was approaching the same age, he was terrified of leaving the child with his own grandparents. The moment was painful, yet it started the journey toward Steven finding healing from his abuse.

Hint 6: Lack of Touch, Sexual Initiation, and Desire

For men who were abused, it's not unusual to associate sexual pleasure with feelings of guilt, so they struggle to stuff that guilt down far enough to be sexually present—if they can be present at all. Some struggle to maintain erections or to ejaculate, even when their abuse experience did not involve any sort of penetration. Such feelings of guilt can also keep a husband from initiating sex with his wife.

WHAT YOU CAN DO TO LOVE HIM THROUGH THIS

It's natural to have lots of questions and worries around a husband's revelation of past abuse. It's at this point that I must offer a word of caution: *Do not reveal* his secret to any non-licensed professionals. His story is his alone to tell, and it should be told only when he's ready. He needs to do this in his own time and at his own comfort level. If you need help managing your emotions regarding your husband's revelations, consider meeting with a licensed counselor who has experience in these matters.

Author and counselor Greg Smalley offers some additional insights:

- Give your husband space to talk about the abuse at his own pace.
- Offer patience and avoid being judgmental.
- Do not ask for details. Let him reveal what he wishes to reveal.
- He might question his sexual attraction based on his body's response to abuse by another man.
- Reassure him that you are with him for the long haul.
- Don't try to "fix him."
- Be realistic regarding what's ahead. Your husband might experience anger, become more distant, or struggle with anxiety as he comes to terms with his experience.
- You can offer to help him find a counselor, but he still needs to make his own appointments.[5]

(A man can also struggle with his masculinity based on the misguided belief that it's somehow not abuse when a boy is abused by a female.)[6]

When speaking with wives and exploring various reasons why their husbands might experience lower desire levels, I'm usually met with surprise when I ask if they know of any abuse in their husbands' pasts. A common response is, "If I had one hundred hints to guess from for my husband's lack of sexual desire, abuse would be the last one on my radar. The possibility grieves me to my core."

We might not want to think about the possibility of abuse, but we shouldn't rule it out. After all, wouldn't you want your husband to love you through the healing process if you had an abuse experience in your past? Wouldn't you want him to demonstrate extraordinary levels of patience as you worked together toward a place of sexually healthy restoration?

If you do learn that your husband experienced abuse in the past, don't lose hope. Our God is a God of restoration and is capable of healing the wounded places in your marriage. As the Bible says in Psalm 147:3, "He heals the brokenhearted and binds up their wounds."

His Interests Are with Someone Else

THE PHRASE *I LOVE YOU, BUT* . . . flows off the end of his tongue. And there you stand, holding your breath. Your inner sense tells you that what's coming next will be incredibly painful. You're only in shock for a moment—before slumping to the floor in a heap of tears the next.

The phrase has many variations, but it often goes something like this:

I love you, but . . . I'm not in love with you.

I love you, but . . . I've found someone else.

I love you, but . . . I want to have an open marriage.

I love you, but . . . I want us to become swingers.

I love you, but . . . I want to bring another person into the bedroom with us.

I love you, but . . . I'm bisexual.

I love you, but . . . I'm gay.

I love you, but . . . I feel like I'm a woman trapped in a man's body.

The versions above are the most common ones I've encountered among the couples I've counseled. I've heard plenty of dubious justifications and lots of faulty reasoning from folks who want to alter their marriage vows, and if we're going to be completely honest, there's nothing in the hollowness of these words that remotely conveys love. *I love you, but* is just an attempt to soften the blow. It lacks any empathy for the person whose heart has just shattered into a thousand pieces.

Instinctively, the listener's initial reaction is fear—blinding fear. The emotional and sexual withdrawal, irritability, melancholy, and spiraling moods you've witnessed in your husband for months (or even years) suddenly make perfect sense. Your marriage, and everything you thought you knew about it, is at once unrecognizable.

Now you're left to ruminate on all those false declarations of *I love you, but* . . . You feel like you're being force-fed something you do not wish to eat. Nothing is okay anymore.

THE SHIFTING STATE OF SEXUALITY

Those who lack a biblical foundation would have us believe that all things sexual are beneficial—that there are no boundaries. But we know from Scripture that we are to put others before ourselves (see Philippians 2:3-4). This would apply to anything that harms someone's physical, emotional, sexual, or spiritual well-being. If he's not seeking biblical wisdom concerning sexual practices, a husband's desire might indeed be directed away from his wife. In this case, it's not because there's anything wrong with her—it's because she isn't open to unbiblical ideas about God's design for sex and about redefining the very nature and identity of her marriage!

So don't fall for that lie—that we can explore sexuality as much as we desire, with no harm to our marriages—whether it comes from him or someone else. Being "open to exploration" won't magically provide a wife with the intimacy she's been missing. It won't give her what she ultimately desires. Instead, she's more likely to experience shame and jealousy than freedom. Please understand that simply exploring new forms of sexual foreplay isn't sinful, nor is trying a different sexual position. But when a husband wants to forsake his marriage vows in pursuit of sinful sexual practices—infidelity, for example, or anything designed to degrade or abuse—he is actually dehumanizing his wife. That single step can strip her of her sense of value for years to come.

How does the Christian wife respond? It begins here: "*You* can alter *your* perspective of a godly marriage, but you are not allowed to alter *mine*. I love you, *and* no thank you. I'm declining your invitation."

The biggest question for many wives in this situation is *How did I not see the signs?* Time and time again I see marriages implode because a husband tries to redefine the biblical directives regarding marital engagement, and the wife capitulates based on a fear of losing security for herself and her children. One or both spouses might believe that inviting a third person into their bedroom will restore life to their marriage, but such sinful experimentation ultimately brings death. When marital agreements shift without open and honest communication, when the relationship welcomes secrets and lies, when unbiblical practices are tolerated or even welcomed, that's when jealousy and insecurity are sure to follow—not sexual freedom or happiness.

And when we add today's conversations about sexual and gender identity into the mix, we also add the prospect of even more difficulties in marriage.

It was not until the early 1960s that the term *gender identity* even entered our cultural vocabulary. Nowadays we have a "gender spectrum" that allows us to choose one category today and another tomorrow.[1] Scripture says that God created us "male and female" (see Genesis 1:27), but in February 2022, Healthline.com somehow created an expanded spectrum that includes *more than fifty* gender identity and expression options.[2]

My empathy today is with the wife who signed on the dotted line to have a traditional Christian marriage yet now lives with a husband who has changed his mind, perspective, and values. In many cases he's also asked his wife to change hers without asking for her opinion on the matter.

It's no longer unusual when a Christian wife calls me, feeling emotionally crushed because her marriage is likely ending. What's more, her belief in traditional marriage is being touted as outdated, stringent, unbending, intolerant, unloving, prudish, and ignorant. On numerous occasions this sort of derogatory language about traditional marriage is tossed my way—both inside and outside the counseling room—often before I've ever uttered a single word about my personal beliefs.

I regularly meet with Christian women who've come to realize that the man they've been sleeping next to for the past ten to fifty years has restructured his sexual, gender, or marital identity without a single word of conversation. When the truth finally comes out, it often happens through little more than a one-minute statement, with no opportunity for further discussion: "I've been denying my happiness," he says, "and who I am and who I believe God has created me to be, through all our years of marriage." Once again the wife is left with a host of questions. First among them: *How did we get here?*

THE *WHYS* ARE HIDDEN . . . MAYBE

Many wives never receive answers to the questions swirling in their minds. Instead, they are left with feelings of anger and betrayal. They're forced to live with uncertainty about their womanhood, not to mention their inability to spot the warning signs in their husbands. More than fifteen years ago, Focus on the Family published an online article titled "My Spouse Struggles with Homosexuality."[3] So many of the warning signs mentioned back then continue to present themselves today (see the list below). Sure, technology has increased the spouse's ability to keep their secret life hidden, but I'm still astonished by how often I hear of secrets revealed through messaging apps. Methods of deception, while certainly more creative nowadays, have not changed all that much.

In a scenario presented in the article, the wife felt an ever-growing uneasiness: *I never saw it coming, even after seven years of marriage.* The author lists some tangible signs that "something is wrong"—signs that often go unrecognized by wives. I've also added a few that I've encountered in my own practice:

- Increased emotional distance
- Decreased interest in sex
- Increased moodiness, irritability, and even rage
- Making slow but significant changes to their physical appearance—losing weight or hiring a personal trainer
- Wearing new clothing in a style you've never seen them wear before
- Working longer hours or taking exorbitant amounts of time to run errands
- Defensiveness when asked about their whereabouts
- Taking phone calls in another room in the middle of the night
- Unexplained charges to your bank account
- Changing phone service providers, or receiving credit card statements from an account you do not recognize

Sometimes knowledge of a husband's identity shift leads to a revelation, as happened with Allyah.

Allyah had a dream—a dream that left her flustered and anxious for days. Just thinking about it kept her awake at night. "I tried to push it back and push it back," she said, "and I couldn't figure out why it deeply disturbed me. Finally, I had to check Facebook and his emails to see if I could put my concerns to rest. I had never before checked up on my husband in twenty-two years of marriage, but I couldn't shake the weight off my chest." Unfortunately, Allyah couldn't shake off the messages and pictures of same-sex porn that she discovered.

Here I want to offer a cautious, loving note to wives: Please do not head down a never-ending rabbit hole. It's not your role to become a private investigator. When the deceit runs deep, it can take years for God to reveal and shed light on the whole story. In the case of the following couple, the full revelation took more than fifteen years.

In September 2021, I remember catching an interview of a Christian children's book author and his wife on the *Today* show.[4] The husband stated to his family after fifteen years of marriage that he was gay. *People* magazine also did an interview with the author, who said he initially believed he was bisexual and explained how this was not a new discovery for him.[5]

What struck me in both interviews was that little was said regarding what the wife experienced—what she *endured*. She mentioned her heartache, sadness, and grief, and how she mourns what can no longer be, but what about how she had the breath knocked out of her when her husband spoke the words that turned her world upside down?

Behind every such story are elements of confusion, deception, and secrecy, but the ever-present narrative is about *what I need to be happy* and *who I really am*. And that's a painful message for a spouse to receive, not to mention the children and other family members. There are no happy endings for the other parties involved when a spouse chooses to forsake their family. The pain is undeniable, and the message presented to the outside world is seldom consistent with what's really going on at home.

DIFFICULT AND PAINFUL DECISIONS

If a husband's first betrayal is with another woman, many Christian wives work to stay in the marriage. They remain for a variety of reasons—love for the man they fell in love with, the good of their children, wanting to be obedient to God, and financial security. If a husband has a second betrayal or serial affairs, the relationship will face more challenges. When the infidelity comes with a disclosure of same-sex attraction, the long-term likelihood of repairing and restoring the marriage becomes even slimmer.

No matter the specifics, the husband is picking fruit from a different tree. How does a wife accept this? The answer is that she shouldn't—not until the marriage is restored to biblical standards. And if you are currently having sex with your straying husband, it's perfectly valid to wonder about the nature of his real or hidden desires when he is with you. It's also valid to establish some strong boundaries—not only for your emotional well-being, but also for your physical safety. Anyone dealing with sexual infidelity needs to consider halting all sexual activity and visiting a doctor for testing of sexually transmitted infections. My point is, both self-protection and calling your spouse back to fidelity and integrity are essential.

Yet I've seen wives sacrifice their emotional, physical, and spiritual well-being by forsaking their boundaries and begging their husbands to stay in the marriage. Because of a sense of immobilizing fear, they will accept whatever he's willing to give or not give. Some will downplay or even deny the warning signs that God has provided. When you feel deep within your being that something is *off*, yet you keep pushing it away, please reconsider.

It is imperative to love yourself enough to say, "No, thank you. I'm not okay with unhealthy behaviors that put our relationship and my well-being at risk."

There is a time when your first priority is not to save the marriage but to lovingly and compassionately care for yourself. Putting your oxygen mask on first is often necessary before you can think about saving your children, your spouse, or your marriage.

Your husband might refuse marital counseling because he doesn't see anything worth saving. It's not unusual to receive such resistance, but it's also okay to say, "I am going to start the process of healing. I hope you will join me in time." The truth is that he *knows* he has hurt you deeply. It's extremely difficult to face our guilt and shame when it's staring us in the face—especially knowing that we willingly caused another human being such pain.

It might take a while, but in time you'll discover whether the marriage is salvageable. Going through Christian counseling together is about accepting God's design for marriage, repenting and offering forgiveness, restoring emotional stability, finding solutions, communicating with empathy, and considering the well-being of any children you have together. Reconciliation does not always lead to the *restoration* of a marriage. Sometimes it simply involves the reconciliation of a brother and sister in Christ. (Focus on the Family counselors have created a resource for wives called *Aftershock: Overcoming His Secret Life with Pornography: A Plan for Recovery*.[6])

If your husband is unwilling to attend counseling, then the best strategy might include waiting. See a counselor by yourself; then ask your husband again once you have gained more confidence in loving yourself and have the renewed strength that comes with establishing healthier boundaries. Focus right now on understanding Christ's love for you. When your earthly husband falls short of loving you well, our heavenly bridegroom is ready to comfort you.

> **Sometimes you have to poke holes in the darkness until it bleeds light.**
>
> MARGARET FEINBERG[7]

There is a refining and redefining process that comes next—one that requires you to move beyond panic mode and trust God for the outcome. You *are* allowed to catch your breath without apology. You *don't* have to make immediate decisions about the future. There are numerous options to weigh and pray about. Take the time you need to process the shock and grief, as well as the potential losses you're facing in the days and months ahead.

Wise decisions are seldom made in moments of immediate pain, but rather over the weeks and months that follow. Some wives choose to remain in a wounded marriage no matter the circumstances, some choose a period of separation (a temporary and structured time apart to gain perspective, release pressure, and reduce destructive anger and conflict), and some ultimately choose divorce.[8]

There is a school of thinking in some Christian circles that encourages spouses to remain in their marriages *no matter what*. Yet this can be emotionally hurtful and even personally dangerous when there is chronic adultery or abuse—when the physical, emotional, and spiritual safety of a woman or her children is at stake. As much as possible, try to avoid merely *reacting* to your circumstances. Be *cautious* instead by continually assessing—with the aid of wise, godly counsel—your specific situation.

Cautionary steps include finding time and space to breathe, slowing down the spiral of your thought life, praying, resting, regaining strength, and setting boundaries. Try to establish a sense of safety and security. Taking the time you need is not selfish; it's necessary for emotional and spiritual growth.

I cannot reiterate enough that a regular, ongoing commitment to Christian counseling with an individual who specializes in this area can help you find a way to put the pieces of your shattered heart back together again. And please get evaluated for depression or anxiety if you find you cannot function in day-to-day life, especially in terms of getting enough sleep, going to work, paying the bills, eating regularly, maintaining good physical hygiene, or caring for children. Getting help is not a sign of weakness, but one of strength.

> For I, the LORD your God,
>   hold your right hand;
> it is I who say to you, "Fear not,
>   I am the one who helps you."
>
> ISAIAH 41:13

10

He Withholds Sex Intentionally

A CRUEL REALITY is that some husbands withhold sex as a form of punishment or as part of a power struggle. This isn't a particularly common scenario when a husband struggles with lower sexual desire or initiation, but when it does happen, the men who employ this tactic tend to be narcissistic and practice covert manipulation. For whatever reason—typically their own shame or need for power—they've decided to emotionally and verbally reinforce the belief that their wives don't deserve affection or the experience of sexual pleasure. (To be fair, both men and women have engaged in such behavior, and it's harmful coming from either spouse.)

Such thinking represents an inaccurate view of Scripture and of God's design for sexuality. A husband's views might involve distorted concepts of submission and of his being the sole sexual initiator and decision-maker, as well as tightly held opinions on gender roles for men and women. (A word of warning here: Some of the stories in this chapter might be highly distressing to women who've experienced domestic abuse.)

These are some of the things I've heard from wives:

Every time I attempt to initiate sex with my husband, I'm told, "Women shouldn't initiate, only men."
JESSICA

I'm not allowed to hug or kiss my husband without asking permission.
CORINNE

My husband and I were working on a bedroom makeover as an anniversary gift to each other. As we were doing a final cleanup, I realized the paint required a few touch-ups. When I mentioned the missed spots with "Hey, honey, we have a few touch-ups to do," my husband picked up the paint tray and threw it across the room. He then refused to have sex with me for six months.
TANISHA

I was a virgin when we married, and we had sex once on our honeymoon. Two years later we've had no further sexual or nonsexual contact. He no longer wants me to touch him.
NATASHA

Abuse can be disguised in a variety of ways that many women are unaware of. The most common forms are psychological/emotional, verbal, and physical abuse. Yet sexual abuse, financial abuse (denying access to family funds), isolation, neglect, and spiritual abuse are also frequently in the mix. At the root of abusive behaviors are dynamics of superiority, prejudice, insecurity, power and control differentials, and rigid gender expectations. According to the National Domestic Violence Hotline, domestic violence—also referred to as intimate partner violence (IPV), dating abuse, or relationship abuse—is a "pattern of behaviors used by one partner to maintain power and control over another partner in an intimate relationship."[1] (To understand more about what constitutes abuse and how to respond, visit **FocusOnTheFamily.com /AbusiveRelationships**.)

Since the scope of this book is sexuality, let's try to understand how power, control, and coercion might show up in this specific area of marriage. First, any *demands* on the part of either partner, including sexual demands, reflect an absence of love. Love does not insist on its own way (see 1 Corinthians 13:5).

Second, if your husband refuses to engage in affection or sexual contact with you based on what he believes sexual pleasure *should* be—unknown by many wives, a husband might act this way because of his own shame tied to viewing distorted, pornographic images of sexual pleasure—this is a huge red flag.

Third, if he hurts you—for example, he slaps or pinches you on the behind (even after you ask him to stop), then he pouts and does it again the next day—it is abusive, and he is dishonoring your boundaries.

Fourth, if you refuse to engage in a sexual or nonsexual encounter because it made you feel uncomfortable or caused physical or emotional pain, and you are *punished* for it by being called prudish or any other derogatory name, this is coercion. Coercion has no place in a Christ-centered marriage. It indicates a mindset of pressure, threat, or force.

It is not unusual for a wife to tell me, "I'd rather do what he wants than not have him touch me at all." Her feelings of sexual deprivation might make this response seem reasonable, but take a moment to think about it. In any one of the four scenarios presented above, a husband's pouting, silent treatment, and emotional and physical withdrawal are never acceptable behaviors in a Christian marriage. To disregard them is to allow them to fester and grow. As we read in Romans 13:10, "Love does no wrong to a neighbor; therefore love is the fulfilling of the law."

A healthy marriage includes the freedom to disagree, to have a different perspective or opinion. This includes the freedom to say, "No, this does not work well for me or make me comfortable." Yes, elements of reasonable sacrifice and considering what the other spouse might desire in the bedroom are part of a marriage's sexual growth and journey. But in a healthy marriage, husbands and wives do not respond to each other with manipulation, coercion, or retaliation to get their way. To behave this way is not consistent with the genuine, gentle, and loving intimacy that God intends.

WHEN INDIFFERENCE IS YOUR COMPANION

Indifference can creep into a marriage and sideswipe a wife with such force that she doesn't know what hit her until the Holy Spirit opens her eyes and she can see again. Angela's story, for example, can help us understand some different aspects of indifference.

ANGELA'S STORY

While on vacation several years ago, our family was driving through a construction zone. A road worker suddenly set a large barrel in front of us—one we were about to hit. My husband did not notice it, so I screamed out, "Careful, do you see him?" He swerved and avoided the barrel and the worker by just a few inches.

Upon arriving at our destination, I realized that if I asked my husband anything, I received brief, curt answers. Over the next several days, I could sense the chill and distance between us. This one incident froze him out emotionally and physically from our children and from me. We are still in this same place several years later. I've said to him, "You seem distant. I've reached for you at night and you've not reached back. I'm concerned about the distance between us. We've had no kisses, hugging, or touching."

The response I received (after several months) was "You emasculated me in front of our kids." When I heard my husband's words, I was floored and searched my soul for how we got to this place. Were there other signs of discord in our relationship? We are now four years into this gridlock, even though I've apologized and asked for forgiveness. I've asked him if we could speak to our pastor or go for marriage counseling, and all I receive are shoulder shrugs. I love my husband, but I don't want to live without affection. I don't deserve four years of what I endured.

Author Leslie Vernick wrote an article for The American Association of Christian Counselors titled "Is Marital Indifference Emotionally Abusive?" in which she describes chronic indifference and its effects. Posted ten years ago, Vernick's words of wisdom still ring true today:

The opposite of love isn't hate, it is indifference. Indifference says I don't care enough about you to give you my time, my energy or other resources to show interest, care, or love towards you. Indifference says how you feel or what you want doesn't matter to me. Indifference says you are not a person to love, but an object to use. Indifference says I don't need to change anything to make our relationship better for you if it's okay for me. Indifference says that you exist for my benefit and when you don't please me or benefit me anymore, you are replaceable or disposable.[2]

Social norms once told us that husbands couldn't be emotionally sensitive. Tough exteriors and tough interiors were how they used to tackle the world. We now know that it's okay for both his interior and exterior to be tender, loving, and caring, but this doesn't mean men aren't still sensitive to perceived messages of inadequacy. I know many husbands who still sometimes emotionally withdraw from their wives or revert to the ways they typically interact with other men.

Let's say that during your last sexual encounter, you mentioned, "Honey, it would feel better for me if you moved over a little bit this way," or "I'd really love it if you would do this." Were you communicating a message of inadequacy regarding his lovemaking skills? Not at all. You aren't automatically criticizing him simply by expressing your desires, but (as I mentioned earlier) you should try to be thoughtful in how you present such requests, because he might perceive them as critical.

And that's when you suddenly find that he's blaming you for diminishing him as a husband or lover. He might decide to withhold sex and punish you for having told him something you needed to add pleasure to your lovemaking. He interprets your request to mean that his efforts are not appreciated, he defends himself in his mind by deciding that you ask for too much, and then he shuts down emotionally. The result? No more intimacy.

Sometimes it gets even worse. He might now choose to use your desire for sex as a weapon against you. "What's wrong with you?" he might say. "Women don't do it this way. Women don't need sex every other day." Next comes the accusation that you're somehow not a *normal* woman. "Why are you asking for more from me?"

Whether or not your spouse realizes it, such words diminish, humiliate, and make you feel *less than*. Treating a spouse this way—especially regarding the extremely sensitive topic of sexuality—is never justifiable. These negative communication patterns need to be broken. Often such harmful words come from a place of pain, insecurity, and old wounds, either in the marriage or from the past. Maybe he's hurting you because he is already hurting. Maybe his hurtful comments are a misguided defense mechanism from an insecure individual.

If a wife learns to spot the difference between when he is trying to humiliate her and when he is trying to protect himself, she can better recognize why he is behaving this way. That's why learning how to have "heart talks" rather than reactively drawing verbal swords is essential. (Creating relational safety and breaking free of reactive communication patterns is a focus of the programs offered at Focus on the Family's Hope Restored marriage intensives. Learn more at **HopeRestored.com**.)

Indifference can be just as painful. Wives compare indifference to being ignored or just plain neglected. The only interaction a wife might have with her indifferent husband is when he leaves for work and comes home. In some situations, his work takes place at a home office, in which case the husband is present physically but absent in the other aspects of family life.

With indifference, conversation is minimal at best. He's no longer there to help care for the children and home or pay the bills. In some cases, he is busy playing video games or watching sports.

I've even heard of cases where the husband won't come to the table for meals, stops caring for the yard, or even forsakes his hygiene. He refuses to make plans for the weekends or for family vacations.

John Gottman, a well-known relationship expert, calls this sort of emotional withdrawal *stonewalling*.[3] It's not as uncommon as you might think. At its most hurtful and damaging, stonewalling in a marriage involves a refusal to cooperate or communicate. Men might shut down simply because they can't figure out a way forward. If they don't know what to do, then sometimes it's easier not to try. But if the behavior is intentional and if it's left unaddressed, it's a form of gaslighting—intentionally sowing confusion in the other partner. Stonewalling tells a wife she is not worth the effort. As one wife described it, "I cease to exist."

Bartering is another form of coercive abuse in which a husband makes a promise for intimacy conditional. As in,

If you give me this, I'll give you . . .
If you let me spend $300 on gaming this week, I'll give you . . .
If you lose fifteen pounds, I'll give you . . .
If you let me buy a new car, I'll give you . . .
If you color your hair blonde and grow it long, I'll give you . . .
If you get your breasts enlarged, I'll give you . . .
If you keep our house cleaner, I'll give you . . .
If you keep the kids quiet and out of my way, I'll give you . . .
If you get a tummy tuck, I'll give you . . .

Bartering is inherently demeaning. It reduces the relationship to one of transaction and manipulation. Sooner or later—usually sooner—the presumed promises of *I'll give you* evaporate. One excuse follows another, and yet another bargain gets added to the pile of pain and rejection as the damage continues to spiral.

FELICIA'S STORY

> You don't know what it's like when you desperately
> hope for physical connection with your husband and
> he outright refuses to provide it. It's gotten to the point
> where I am completely discouraged by his treatment
> and neglect. I'm torn down to a place where I no longer
> believe I'm beautiful. Even if he did have a change of
> heart, I'm not sure I'd want him to touch me anymore.
> I can no longer be vulnerable because I believe that any
> further scorn will destroy me completely. I'm done trying
> to change myself into something I'm not. Done. I'm
> beginning to believe that he wants me to look like his
> favorite "secret" porn star. You know—the porn he keeps
> denying. The porn he doesn't look at. I'm hanging on to
> my marriage by a thread.

You know when the poor treatment you receive doesn't feel right, because it distorts who God created you to be as a spouse. You may recognize this when you step away from an interaction with your husband feeling as though you are not his partner but his *less than*.

In all of Jesus' interactions with women—particularly the Samaritan woman at the well (see John 4:4-26) and the woman about to be stoned (see John 8:1-11)—the intent was to redeem and lift up each woman out of less-than status and to demonstrate love and mercy to her.

Jesus doesn't make anyone feel less than. He extends His love and mercy to all.

If you continually walk away from interactions with your husband feeling punished, you need to know that this is not the way of Christ. If your husband is unwilling to listen to your concerns about intimacy and instead chooses to react with defensiveness and blame, that's *never* your fault. You're not wrong to expect an open, honest, and non-escalating conversation about what's occurring in your marriage. You're not wrong to expect a respectful discussion about what is hurtful and requires attention.

And if indifference and stonewalling remain the norm in your marriage, there are much more serious issues taking place that should not be ignored.

An ongoing pattern of these behaviors can rightly be considered abusive. Don't be hesitant or feel shame about seeking professional help in assessing your situation. You might need to hear this: If abuse is occurring, it should never be condoned. Moreover, it requires *individual* counseling for both you and your husband.

In other words, addressing abuse in a marriage does *not* begin with traditional couples therapy. The manipulated, mistreated, or bullied spouse needs to first seek competent care individually so the matter can be safely assessed and then safely addressed. Such matters are not just marriage issues, but are *individual* issues that affect the marriage.

In these circumstances, it's vital to begin with pursuing individual healing, which in some instances could require a period of separation. Please note that this is not the sort of open-ended separation that creates a very high potential for divorce. What's recommended instead is something called a *healing separation*—one that is best navigated with a trained pastor or counselor.[4]

A healing separation is very intentional and specific, and it involves agreed-upon steps that help create emotional, physical, and spiritual safety. There are rules, accountability, and check-ins—all designed to assist in restoring the relationship. Creating space is often necessary, but the goal remains to eventually move the relationship toward marriage counseling and reconciliation.

The purpose of individual counseling, meanwhile, is to help both spouses gain insight and growth regarding dysfunctional patterns and to discern whether there is genuine heart change, remorse, and behavioral changes that include establishing a track record of rebuilding trust. Safety is always the priority. This might involve a long-term or even permanent separation. Working to forgive is important, but rebuilding trust in your relationship is a different story.

While working on your own healing, you'll likely discover there are aspects of your own thinking and behaviors that are unhealthy and, quite frankly, far from Christlike. Maybe you believe that God can't or won't help change your husband. *He's the one who needs changing, not me.* Maybe you've spent so much time thinking and talking negatively about your husband to others that you've become filled with bitterness and resentment—perhaps to the point that you hardly recognize yourself in the mirror.

What happens when you get to the point where you believe nothing will ever change? That's what we'll examine next.

11

He Doesn't Live Up to My Expectations

IF YOU'RE ALREADY HURTING from feelings of rejection, it's not a stretch to find yourself struggling with a mindset known as *he never and he always*. This mindset assumes that you are the ideal spouse . . . and he's not. *He never gives me what I need. He always puts himself first.*

But if you're going to assume anything, the best place to begin is recognizing that neither one of you came into marriage without flaws. The predicament with a *he never and he always* mindset is that all the focus is on his shortcomings and none of the focus is on your own. We keep looking for change in the other person's heart, even when our own heart could use some chiseling.

If you are reading this book, then you've likely experienced sexual rejection for reasons you do not understand. And because of that heartache, you might feel spiritually justified in speaking your pain out loud, even if the words are unkind. If that's the case, then Scripture provides great wisdom in helping us examine the flaws in our attitudes toward our husbands:

> Death and life are in the power of the tongue, and those who love it will eat its fruits.
>
> PROVERBS 18:21

> Watch the way you talk. Let nothing foul or dirty come out of your mouth. Say only what helps, each word a gift.
>
> EPHESIANS 4:29, MSG

> If you bite and devour one another, watch out that you are not consumed by one another.
>
> GALATIANS 5:15

There is power in the messages that a wife conveys—both verbally and nonverbally—and they will either draw her husband toward her or push him away. A man can sense when his wife exhibits her displeasure with him. You might think you're keeping these thoughts to yourself, but he knows that *he never* measures up to your expectations, or that *he's always* inadequate in meeting your standards as a man. The "*he never* meets my standards" and "*he always* falls short" message can kill a husband's sex drive in the blink of an eye.

The worse things get and the longer this sexual disconnection

> We need to realize our need for limits because we need to submit ourselves to the same rules we want our partner to submit to.
>
> HENRY CLOUD[1]

continues, a wife can become so disappointed that she attempts to control not only her husband, but the entire relationship. This can lead to a lack of admiration of and appreciation for *everything* he contributes to the financial, emotional, physical, and spiritual health of the home.

When a wife's heart is filled with bitterness and resentment, she veers off a healthy path. She also develops the potential to engage in emotional, verbal, or spiritual harm—even abuse—against her husband. And when that happens, the woman who thinks poorly of her husband can find herself changing into someone she swore she would never become.

NICKOLAS'S STORY

Since I was diagnosed with diabetes, I'm doing everything I can to watch my diet and glucose levels, but my body does not always respond during lovemaking like it used to because of this disease. I'm told I'm a lazy lover and less than a man. After the first time my body didn't respond, I was accused of cheating. She tells me that if I were in tune with her, I would know her needs without her stating them.

I love my wife but I can't read her mind. I can't seem to put my underwear in my dresser drawer correctly, or I fold the laundry like an idiot. I'm deeply committed to my marriage as a man of God, but I can't go on like this. I can no longer bear to hear a sentence that starts with "Other men . . ."

I feel I'm present in every way to show up and parent our kids, help with baths and homework, partner in the housework, make meals, grocery shop, pay bills, and keep up with the yard. I work every day to meet her where she needs me to be spiritually as the head of our home, but I can't even pray the right way. I'm finding it more difficult each day to actually want to kiss her.

Unfortunately, Nickolas is not the first husband and father to share this type of story with me. "I have no desire," he says, "to kiss a mouth that tells me I do nothing right."

Several years ago, while at a picnic, I observed a wife pat her husband's stomach and say, "You think you've had enough to eat today?" I cringed as this man turned red and walked away without a word. He spent the rest of the afternoon playing with the kids. He no longer even engaged in conversation with the other men at the picnic.

Do you think there was much chance of this couple sharing an intimate moment later that evening? Imagine your husband saying those words to you in front of a group of friends. I can't imagine it, but I know it happens.

When a wife tries to mold and shape her husband into some idealized image rather than encouraging the gifts and talents that God gave him, he is extremely likely to withdraw sexually. And the further he steps away to protect himself, the harder she'll try to get him to respond—many times with harsh or unloving words. The ongoing cycle of unmet needs and expectations is like a perpetually spinning hamster wheel, with neither spouse receiving what they truly desire in terms of sexual and emotional connection.

CHANGE YOUR WORDS, CHANGE THE ENVIRONMENT

For dramatic healing to occur in your marriage, shifting your words toward building up rather than tearing down can make a world of difference. Instead of looking for things the other person is doing wrong, try to catch each other doing things well. For your marriage to flourish, the verbal shredding of each other's hearts must stop.

Own the baggage that each of you brings to the table. Demonstrate sorrow and remorse. Seek forgiveness. Otherwise you'll keep repeating the same scenarios of blame and shame—*You did it. It's your fault. You never* and *You always.*

It's your choice.

Wives: You can create a healthy verbal and emotional atmosphere in your marriage. You can model change to your husband. After creating Adam, the Lord said, "I will make him a helper [one who balances him—a counterpart who is] suitable and complementary for him" (Genesis 2:18, AMP). We are not without responsibility in helping our relationship flourish during the most challenging seasons.

Tim Alan Gardner, author of *Sacred Sex*, writes, "When you allow thoughts that are critical or demeaning, no matter how slight, to fill your head, they will kill your passion."[2] As women, we desire to be valued, but we need to recognize that value is also something our husbands desire from us. Mutual expressions of worth are essential in creating a healthy marriage environment.

> We never go wrong in connecting with our spouse if our words and behaviors are filled with kindness and patience.

No *one* has sole responsibility for creating a vibrant and passionate atmosphere in a marriage. It does not lie only in a husband's hands or only in the wife's. Demonstrating kindness, concern, value, and mutual respect—as well as prioritizing the marriage over children, work, or self—can make a world of difference in cultivating a thriving relationship.

Authors Linda Dillow and Lorraine Pintus put it this way: "Passion begins with priorities, not genitals. . . . Sex isn't an event, it's an environment."[3]

In the pages to come, we'll continue to learn about reframing passion when his desire is absent. We'll also come back to the question of where passion begins.

UNPACKING THE PAST

We're not quite done examining long-held beliefs about what constitutes genuine manliness. We still need to contemplate a tough question:

Do I set him up in my mind for success in our marriage—or for failure as my husband?

As we shift toward a healthier cultural mindset about the role of men, we might have to get rid of some boxes that our parents, siblings, coworkers, and friends have unknowingly added to the corners of our bedrooms. In *Not Always in the Mood: The New Science of Men, Sex, and Relationships*, sex researcher Sarah Hunter Murray advocates for abolishing what she calls the "bro code"— outdated and misguided views about desire that many of us picked up along the journey toward marriage.

The following are a few myths Murray addresses, as well as ones I hear frequently in conversations with Christian wives.[4] Remember, these are myths we are working to dispel:

- A man's sexual desire is high and unwavering.
- Men are the ones who do the desiring.
- Men don't need to feel desirable themselves.
- Men are the pursuers and should initiate all sexual activity.
- Sexual rejection doesn't hurt. Men are used to it and even expect it.

My immediate response is "Who says men are like this?" My take on such "bro codes" is that they make many men—particularly husbands—feel like failures when they fail to conform. Consequently, the code also compels women to bring boxes of disappointment into the bedrooms they share with their husbands.

Sarah Hunter Murray opened my eyes to my own biases regarding a man's capacity for desire (or lack thereof). For several years I've been saving emails and stories from hurting and frustrated women who have higher desire levels than their husbands, and Murray points out how little research has been done on this topic. I started seeing her articles and research about ten years ago, and I learned how she began reevaluating her own beliefs about men and desire.

To help put the research disparity in perspective, predominantly male researchers have been studying low desire in women for several decades. No wonder social norms for years put couples into the same pursuer/pursued relationship box—a box that long reinforced unrealistic expectations for both men and women.

If I haven't already convinced you, it's time to unpack the past and throw many of those boxes into a bonfire. It's time to look to God's Word for our guidance on sexual expectations.

There's a special gem tucked into the Old Testament between Ecclesiastes and Isaiah. Virtually all Christians are aware of this book, yet how many of us are familiar with this series of poetic lyrics and songs about the love between Solomon and a Shulammite woman in Song of Solomon? And how many of us have taken time to study its meaning and application for us today?

As I was working on this book, I sent out several *inquiring-minds-want-to-know* sorts of questions regarding Christian perspectives on sex. The responses from family, friends, and colleagues were surprising. One in particular astounded me: "Song of Solomon is pure fantasy; marriage and passion can't be like this."

I wholeheartedly beg to differ.

There is no other place in God's Word that so clearly reveals His design for sexuality between husband and wife. There is no other place that so clearly describes how mutual pursuit—rather than one-sided pursuit—is holy, beautiful, and healthy. Romantic devotion is likewise depicted as mutual. It's a wonderful representation of devotion to God and His design for sexuality.

The Shulammite woman passionately pursues Solomon using her words, eyes, and body. Their relationship is not one-sided, which itself is a deviation from the tropes that say the man is supposed to handle the heavy lifting of pursuit. But don't take it from me. Read the woman's words to her lover for yourself:

"May he kiss me with the kisses of his mouth!
For your love is sweeter than wine."
SONG OF SOLOMON 1:2, NASB

"Like an apple tree among the trees of the forest,
So is my beloved among the young men.
In his shade I took great delight and sat down,
And his fruit was sweet to my taste."
SONG OF SOLOMON 2:3, NASB

"His thighs are pillars of alabaster
Set on pedestals of pure gold."
SONG OF SOLOMON 5:15, NASB

"His mouth is full of sweetness.
And he is wholly desirable."
SONG OF SOLOMON 5:16, NASB

That said, I understand that for most readers of this book, the problem is not your pursuit of your husband, but rather that he has stopped pursuing *you*. You want—need—to know *why*. One answer might be tied to the connection between your thoughts and words regarding him. Are desire-giving or desire-draining words spilling out?

ACKNOWLEDGING YOUR OWN RESPONSIBILITY

I might as well acknowledge the obvious right here: I expect readers to feel a bit uncomfortable as they chew on this chapter. The anger, disappointments, and resentments stemming from the struggles in your marriage probably have you looking for a way to vent your frustrations.

While there are likely plenty of issues that rest primarily in our husbands' laps, that's not the case all the time. There is a certain percentage that we need to own as wives. We're certainly not perfect, thus we need to own 100 percent of the responsibility for the aspects that we control. Let's be honest: We don't always get it right. We don't always treat our husbands lovingly. Ask yourself:

- Do I actively show him that he is a priority in my life?
- Do 101 other things come ahead of him on my perpetual to-do list?
- In the course of our marriage, have I always tried to say yes to his advances?
- Are there times when I've said no, and he's felt rejected?

Authentically and honestly acknowledge the elephant in the room: your own role in your marriage. Consider the part that *you* play in these issues. Sit with yourself for a while and become acquainted with the real you. No one has an ideal home, an ideal spouse, ideal children, or an ideal marriage. This includes me. Let me give you an example of my own mistake in preferring perfectionism.

SHERI AND JIM'S STORY

For our anniversary last year we purchased new bedding and pillows. Most of the time my loving husband makes the bed in the morning, but he wasn't putting the new pillows on the bed the right way. One pillow has decorative birds; if placed incorrectly (upside down), the birds appear dead with their feet up in the air. I noticed my irritation growing, and I started going back to the bedroom after he made the bed and fixing everything myself.

One morning, when Jim asked for more than our usual morning kiss on the lips, I turned to give him my cheek instead. Puzzled, he finally asked, "What's up? Did I make the bed wrong?"

I blurted out, "Don't you even notice that the birds died? How can I be intimate with a man who is so oblivious?"

I stood there stunned at my own response. Honestly, I sometimes fall very short with the words that flow out of my mouth.

Jim was hurt and visibly withdrew. I had some sincere apologizing to do that morning.

This story is an example of the elephant in the room. We don't want to think about or treat our husbands poorly—especially if they haven't actually done anything wrong! Wives, our thoughts and behaviors can be incredibly subtle yet incredibly powerful (and hurtful). At lightning speed, our words and actions can help improve or break the emotional and physical connection we have with our husbands. Yes, it can happen that fast.

We need moments of grace from our husbands, and they need the very same from us.

PART THREE

Solutions

12

What Didn't Work Before Surely Won't Work Again

IF YOU'RE LIKE A LOT OF WIVES, you've tried a variety of tactics—pleading, crying, shaming, guilting—in an effort to get what you want. But they haven't worked, and you don't understand why. Likely without realizing it, your approach has become *He's pushing me away, so I'll pursue him more*. As a result, you end up (unintentionally) *pushing him away*.

When we do this, we end up keeping the relationship at a distance. We've seen him become cold toward us, and we respond by going cold toward him. We grieve, but not well, thus bitterness and resentment grow. There is an alternative—responding and reacting in ways that shed light and love on the situation through seeking God's Spirit to help us pursue patience, kindness, self-control, and gentleness. The process might sound simple, but these are extremely daunting steps when we're in pain.

Authors and relationship experts Les and Leslie Parrott write, "A satisfying marital sex life is a two-way street. It takes both spouses working together to create intimacy and closeness."[1] That's the crux of the situation, isn't it? A healthy marital sex life requires communication and vulnerability from *both* spouses. But who is willing to demonstrate the necessary vulnerability? For many of you reading this book, my guess is that, in your marriage, neither spouse is ready to demonstrate vulnerability—at least not right now.

We want good things when we want them. But when we come at them from broken places, we react in wrong ways and end up hurting the people we love. Do we ever step back and think, *Do I really want to hurt the person I love?* No, we don't really want to do that, yet our actions suggest otherwise.

> We want good things when we want them. But when we come at them from broken places, we react in wrong ways.

What didn't work previously and surely won't work moving forward is keeping the issue of desire differences—and your own feelings of rejection—hidden away. We've long kept this secret stuffed in a storage locker, concerned with how we might be perceived as an imperfect wife with an imperfect marriage. How is that strategy working for you so far?

You say you're an imperfect wife with an imperfect husband? Well, welcome to marriage! The imperfections in your relationship (and mine!) began the moment we walked back up the aisle together. A critical early step in grieving the sexual desire differences in your marriage is to recognize that you and your husband don't live in an enchanted forest.

If you're not already aware of the grieving process, it goes something like this:

- We *deny* to ourselves the truth of what's happening.
- We get *angry* about what is happening.
- We try to *bargain* in our minds. *If only I had done this, things would be better. If only I had done that, he would have changed.* It doesn't work—it only postpones the hurt.
- We get *depressed* when we see the truth about what's happening.
- Finally, we *accept* the truth about our situation. *Is this my new reality?*

Many times, the process of examining, digging deep, and moving through the stages of grief works best with the help of trained experts—both mental and physical health professionals. Sometimes there will be a very clear reason why his body doesn't respond or why his desire for sex is less than yours. Sometimes it's a matter of finding contentment—of accepting that he is simply wired to want sex less than you, in which case you should concentrate on healthy communication regarding this desire discrepancy. And sometimes, maybe after trying every tactic and test, there is no answer other than prayer. Maybe that's simply where his mind and body are *right now.* There will be times when he responds, and there will be times when he doesn't.

When that reality becomes clear, the sad truth is that I hear women across the faith spectrum declare, "If we can't have intercourse, then I can't stay married."

This all-or-nothing mindset is a big step toward catastrophic thinking, and it's deeply unhelpful. (Imagine what some would think—or say—about a man who abandoned his wife because she didn't want, or couldn't participate in, sex as often as he preferred.)

Consider for a moment that with this attitude, the ultimate success or failure of your marriage rests on one body part working at full capacity—on demand. I know of women at all faith levels who have stepped away from their marriages because of a husband's struggle with erectile dysfunction (ED). And most of these women have little to no knowledge about how the male body works or doesn't work.

Writing for Medical News Today, health and wellness journalist Jenna Fletcher says, "Many factors that contribute to ED can occur at any age. . . . Age is a main risk factor for ED. According to some estimates, males have a 40% chance of having some form of ED by their forties. The risk then increases about 10% per decade."[2]

Many wives I speak with believe ED only happens to older men. When I first entered the counseling field, this was a topic I never imagined discussing with women about their husbands. Then again, I've also had to reframe my own thinking and learn that my husband is not Superman all day, every day.

GOD PLANTED AN IDEA

It was nearly a decade ago when I saved my first email from a Christian wife who was hurting over the desire differences in her marriage. She looked forward to lovemaking several times a month, while her husband was a few-times-a-year kind of guy. I've saved and prayed over every note I've received since that first email.

Nearly every wife who reached out to me asked me to tell the Christian community that they are tired of reading about how men are the only ones who deal with a low-desire spouse. Wives are tired of hearing that the sexual issues in marriage are usually their fault.

If things are going well, the women I heard from had noticed, the husband typically receives the credit. But if things are going poorly, it's almost always *her* problem. She's the one who needs to *try a little harder*. These wives say they are tired of talking to pastors and lay leaders who seldom tell their husbands to *try a little harder*. These brave women asked me to share their challenges regarding desire differences with others in the Christian arena. Little did I know that, a few years later, challenges would arise in my own marriage. I trusted that it was God's timing . . . but I was not amused.

A STORY OF GOD WORKING

My husband, Jim, often goes through a few months of seasonal blues each year. He's not a big fan of the gray winter days in Chicago. For some reason, one particular winter led to a deeper bout of depression than normal and a greater understanding of seasonal affective disorder. The medications his doctors prescribed had numerous side effects, and I watched his normally fun and mischievous personality disappear. They also robbed my husband's body of all its physical and sexual energy.

We met with doctors and discussed various medication options, but nothing changed for a long while. Depression showed up in our home as an unwelcome guest. I wasn't used to "I'm tired," "I don't feel like it," or "You're asking too much of me"—not to mention the nonverbal communication: heavy sighs, shoulder shrugs, eye rolls, and turning away in bed at night without a word.

I was angry. I was bitter. I was devastated. Most of all I was lonely. My desires weren't being met, and this girl wanted answers *now*.

Many women have shared similar experiences with me. Sadly, some have experienced even more hurtful moments with their husbands. Ongoing mental health issues can drain the energy out of both partners. Then there are those moments, just when you felt like things were finally improving, when you slowly watch the symptoms come creeping back.

Several doctors had to deal with a very frustrated wife as Jim tried one medication after another with no significant improvements. For what felt like an eternity, I cried out to God and begged Him to take Jim's depression away—to restore the intimacy and playfulness in my marriage. I must admit that I was more focused on results and less on my devoted husband's heart.

Then one morning, while I was sitting at my desk in tears, it seemed like God tapped me on the shoulder. Actually, that tap felt more like a shove. Although God's prompting was gentle, He brought back to me a powerful memory.

I was reminded of another time of desire differences from many years ago, when this same man stood beside me for five years—through six surgeries, a full hysterectomy, and crazy mood swings with hormone adjustments after the birth of our youngest daughter. My husband went with me to numerous doctor appointments, loved me through every moment, remained faithful to his vows, and found new ways to explore sexuality with me.

I can't accurately describe this moment with the Lord as a conversation, because it was extremely one-sided. There's nothing like receiving a massive dose of loving truth!

The following morning, while reading in 1 Corinthians, I received one more reminder of how my husband and I are part of one body in Christ—and Christ is whom we love and serve together in our marriage. One particular passage helped wash away any remaining tears, anger, and resentment:

> There are many parts, yet one body.
> The eye cannot say to the hand, "I have no need of you," nor again the head to the feet, "I have no need

of you." On the contrary, *the parts of the body that seem to be weaker are indispensable,* and on those parts of the body that we think less honorable we bestow the greater honor, and our unpresentable parts are treated with greater modesty, which our more presentable parts do not require. But God has so composed the body, giving greater honor to the part that lacked it, that there may be no division in the body, but that the members may have the same care for one another. If one member suffers, all suffer together; if one member is honored, all rejoice together.

I CORINTHIANS 12:20-26, EMPHASIS ADDED

I realized that I needed to apologize to my best friend and lover for how poorly I'd treated him with my thoughts and words during this time in our marriage. (There are still some times when seasonal depression creeps back into our lives, and I feel it's important to say that Jim gave me permission to share this part of our story.)

The story of my marriage is still being written, but I continue to see God as a merciful healer. I've come to understand that healing often occurs over a series of moments and rarely all at once. And that can be infuriating at times. That's why I pray you continue to feel His presence and comfort no matter the current state of your own desire journey. For all I know, you might want to burn this book in your fireplace while you mutter, "This all sounds great for you, Sheri, but I'm sitting here with no precious healing from a so-called merciful God."

I realize that some marriages might never enjoy a restored sex life. I hear you. I get it. But maybe you can enjoy *something*. If you're experiencing zero intimacy now, with professional help things might improve 5 percent next month and 10 percent the following month. (I'd love to offer you higher numbers, but desire differences tend to ebb and flow depending on numerous internal and external factors—some of which are likely yet to be uncovered and discussed in your marriage.)

And even if your sexual desire issues only improve by 15 percent, isn't that still better than zero intimacy?

MOVING FORWARD

At this point there are several questions I'd like you to reflect on. I, too, considered these questions during the season of desire difference in my own life, and since I'm far from the ideal godly woman and wife, I often found myself wanting to light them on fire or spit them out completely:

- Do I accept that all marriages have seasons of desire difference?
- Is it possible that I am too narrowly focused on my husband's sexuality and capacity to love me based on only one part of his anatomy?
- Has this one part of my husband's body become an idol of sorts in my life? Am I seeing it as my only source of passion or sexual and emotional satisfaction?
- Am I open to learning and exploring sexuality through options other than intercourse?
- Am I open to understanding and learning more about a man's physical, emotional, and mental health?
- Am I willing to talk with doctors or counselors to grow in my knowledge—and am I open to having my husband join me in these conversations?
- Am I still committed to my marriage vows of "in sickness and in health" and "for better and for worse"?

- Am I open to letting the fruit of the Spirit—love, joy, peace, patience, kindness, goodness, faithfulness, gentleness, and self-control—work in and through me (see Galatians 5:22-23)?
- The million-dollar question: What desires and expectations am I willing to leave at the foot of the cross?

Scripture tells us not to fear; the Lord is our help (see Isaiah 41:13). Yet you might be at odds with God much of the time because of your fears or because He's asking you to wait for His response. Waiting is not something that most of us like, and our fears tell us that we need to be in control.

> Get me out of the way, Lord, so You can do the work in our marriage.

I encourage my clients to consider journaling each day. Use this time to examine something you're grateful for, someone or something you admire, a highlight of your day, what you're looking forward to, and one thing you have learned. You might also wrestle with and pray about the questions listed above.

If you have a trusted female Christian friend, mentor, or small group leader who you know can keep a confidence, ask her to support you in prayer. As I cautioned earlier, be careful not to share personal, intimate details about your husband's performance. (Again, I haven't revealed any private matters in this book without Jim's permission. A husband who finds out that personal details are being shared with others might feel humiliated and shut down even further.)

Women of God, we need to share our struggles, but we need to be careful about how we do so. When we ask for prayer, we don't need to include lots of details that are unnecessary and can lean toward gossip. I have no concerns if you say, "Please pray that we can overcome intimacy barriers in our marriage." But telling a family member about your specific bedroom challenges is off limits. This is an area where we should exercise considerable caution.

We want to stop suffering in silence, but we also need to respect our spouses. I'll admit that it can be tricky to find the balance at times. After all, we need to speak—not from a desire to shame, but from a desire to find empathy. We need no longer feel alone. We need not hide the sexual desires that God created, but we can talk about them without sharing the intimate details. If in doubt, don't reveal personal secrets to anyone who isn't professionally bound to keep them.

Even if the only thing you do for a while is request prayer without sharing details, you can trust that God knows the specifics. He knows our needs when others do not. What we don't want is to keep perpetuating outdated narratives about how men and women are "supposed to operate" sexually. So let's keep asking this question: "Who says so?"

13

It's Not Just *His* Issue

DESIRE DISCREPANCY IN MARRIAGE isn't just a *him* or *her* issue. And it isn't a *me* issue either. Differences in sexual desire, as with many struggles in marriage, is an *us* issue. Neither you nor your husband should be left to tackle the issue alone.

Even if you are forced to begin the process alone, the ultimate goal is for couples to work together. Until you and your spouse can attend counseling or medical or psychiatric appointments together, change and restoration will be harder to come by. This struggle requires that you fight for, rather than against, each other. Your husband isn't the enemy. Neither are you. Seek out middle ground. Work to understand each other's fears, wants, and desires. Taking on this struggle together, with cooperation and respectful communication, will go a long way toward restoring more intimacy to the relationship.

The pushback I often hear is "But it's our sex life, and the topic is embarrassing." In response, I encourage you to deal with this issue much like you would an illness. You would tackle it together, right? A kidney stone might feel embarrassing to some, but you still wouldn't drop your spouse off at the emergency room door and leave. If you're both hurt in a car accident, you wouldn't leave your spouse at the hospital as soon as your own injuries were treated.

Instead, let your husband know that he has your support, that he shouldn't feel alone, and that you are committed to working through this issue together. Be a *listener* first and an *encourager* second. *Doer* is much further down the list.

Yet your husband might not be eager to address the issue. He might say, "No, thank you" or "Not yet." It might be painful to you, but your husband could be perfectly content right where he is. At this point there might be nothing more you can do than breathe, step away for a time, and stop trying to convince him otherwise. I know that's a helpless feeling—one that demands faith and one that requires you to leave your husband in God's trustworthy hands.

We all feel helpless at times in life—too paralyzed to make decisions or take next steps. In the same way, when we put the entire burden of our desire discrepancy concerns on our husband, there's a good chance he could feel paralyzed by fear. He's likely feeling awful without knowing why. What he doesn't want is to be perceived as weak—not by you, and not by others. That's why his "No, thank you" or "Not yet" responses come as no surprise.

ROSA'S PATIENCE

Rosa only checked in with her husband about once a month, mostly so he didn't feel pressured. Instead, Rosa felt like she needed to watch, wait, and trust God's timing. She would say to him, "I love you. I'm concerned with our disconnection and how I see you struggling. I have one ask: Can we make an appointment with your doctor to ask him some questions—questions about medications, side effects, blood tests, next steps, and continuing down the discovery trail?"

Eight months later, Rosa's husband thanked her for waiting. He was now ready to move forward.

If your husband doesn't want you to advocate, then begging, pleading, or trying to force him won't do any good. At this point you're looking at a potential power struggle over who's right and who's wrong, along with a competing desire to control and to fix. Don't let that happen. Give your discouragement to God. Ask Him to hold and comfort you. Allow your words to live in your husband's thoughts for a while. Let God do some of the convincing instead of you. Keep in mind that this might involve waiting for quite a while and that there are no guarantees.

If it's been a while and you want to say something, you might try this sort of approach: "Hey, honey. Remember the conversation we had last month about making a doctor appointment? Have you given that any more thought? If you're still unsure, could we pray about it together or brainstorm some options we could explore?"

> My help comes from the LORD, who made heaven and earth.
>
> PSALM 121:2

What you don't want to do is make this approach a daily occurrence. Instead of constant reminders to your husband, concentrate on seeking the Lord. Remain in prayer. Write your prayers down and maybe read them aloud. Maybe it's time to get (prayerfully) vulnerable with each other if that's what it takes for a breakthrough. Look to God in the face of uncertainty and ask Him for what you need.

Seek the Holy Spirit's guidance together. Ask the Lord this question: *Where do You want us to go with this?* If your husband is willing, ask him to sit in silence with you for a few minutes. Focus on one thing you're willing to try over the next month.

Next, engage in discussions that require hearing on your part. Listen to your husband's fears, and try to respond with patience and kindness. Avoid launching verbal volleys like "Why can't you?" "Why don't you?" "Why aren't you?" and "Why haven't you?" No one benefits from this approach because all these queries are tied to unknowns, and "why" questions are often met with defensiveness.

"Love bears all things, believes all things, hopes all things, endures all things" (1 Corinthians 13:7). Love keeps trying. And the more your husband knows you are willing to walk beside him as his life partner, the more he might be willing to do what it takes to make things better.

WHAT IF HE'S NOT WILLING TO TRY—AT LEAST NOT YET?

It's important to step back and acknowledge some of the *him* issues addressed earlier, such as pornography addiction, infidelity, insecurities, and controlling behaviors—any of which might mean you hit a brick wall of resistance. In fact, you should probably expect it.

Let's say that you've done a sincere examination of your own heart and have reached out to your husband in a loving and caring way. You've brought your hurts to him and attempted to work toward understanding and biblical restoration in your marriage. If you've done these things and still nothing has changed, then it's time to seek assistance outside the walls of your home.

Find out if your church has anyone with specific training. There might be pastors or elders with experience in this area, or the church might have a recommendation. Ask your husband to join you. If he won't join you, then don't be afraid to begin the process alone. And don't hesitate to see a Christian counselor on your own if you haven't done so already—with the hope that your husband will eventually accompany you as you work toward healing and restoration.

TALKING TO THE WRONG PEOPLE WON'T BRING SATISFACTION

While many women won't seek help because of their shame and guilt surrounding this issue, they might release their frustrations and anger in other ways. They might bad-mouth their husbands with their girlfriends, sisters, or mothers—the exact people they *shouldn't* talk to about their sex life. Family members and friends often feel compelled to commiserate with and fiercely defend you rather than speak the truth in love about the less-than-stellar heart condition they might see in you. Dealing with a bedroom situation by sharing your every criticism and frustration will never bring happiness or a loving resolution.

One newly married wife shared with her mother her concerns about a lack of intimacy in her marriage and wondered aloud whether it was okay that she wanted sex more often than her husband. She asked her mom to keep their discussion confidential. Yet during the Christmas season, while the family gathered for a cookie-making extravaganza, her mom took a rolling pin, pointed it at her daughter's husband, and said, "Son, you need to give my daughter more loving."

The wife was mortified, of course, and her husband was devastated.

If we fail to go to the right people for support, there's a good chance that we'll feel like we're in court. The husband ends up on the witness stand, where he attempts to defend himself and his actions, while others act as judge, jury, or prosecuting attorneys. Just as no one wants to go on trial, nothing good comes out of the desire-discrepancy courtroom.

The courtroom sends a message to the jury—in this case, our friends and family—that we're either flawed, broken, or guilty. Two things are missing in this courtroom: grace and mercy. And if your marriage does end up on public trial, the verdict is rarely the one you want.

> **Listen to advice and accept instruction, that you may gain wisdom in the future.**
> PROVERBS 19:20

When you seek out the right people—safe, knowledgeable professionals with whom you can share your struggles and tears and who will keep your confidence and offer wise biblical perspectives—you have a much better chance of finding the strength you need to continue the journey toward healing and hope.

CHARYSE'S STORY

I've been married for twenty-three years and I have a husband who is extremely stubborn. He tells me that we can work this out on our own—that our stuff is private. We haven't been intimate in more than fifteen years. What do I do with that response?

If you are the only one making an effort, you've likely figured out by now that you won't be successful on your own. It's good to express your love to your husband, but you can also clearly state that you don't expect your marriage to improve if you're forced to continue tackling the issues by yourself. You need more concrete solutions—and cooperation—in order to feel connection and love.

Don't make guilt-inducing comments such as "Why won't you help us get better?" Commit to the journey for your own well-being; don't put it off hoping things will somehow improve if you keep waiting a little longer.

Let's be honest here. I know what you *want* to say is "Hubby, wake up! Get with the program if you want a happy marriage!" Yet I need to be clear: Scripture doesn't give Christians the option to forsake our marriage vows if our sexual desires aren't met. Marriage is about more than sex, of course, and you might need to accept that this issue won't be resolved to your satisfaction. At that point you'll need to make peace with having less sex—maybe a lot less sex—than you'd like. (You might not want to hear this right now, but consider this question: What would you think if a *man* in your church left his wife solely based on a lack of sex in their marriage?)

But for now, here's an idea: Turn to your husband, look him in the eye, softly touch both shoulders, and say, "I love you, but I do not see us getting better on our own. I don't think our marriage is as good as it could be right now. Please hear me—I don't think our marriage is broken, but what I am asking is that you join me as my partner."

All of this sounds good, some of you are probably thinking, *but it doesn't provide the answers I'm looking for. It won't change him into the lover I deserve.* Well, *change* and *deserve* are two extremely loaded words—two parts of an ultimatum if there ever was one. *Change* that is demanded is not love, and ultimatums often backfire. The more you point out how and where he falls short, the more likely it is that you will get defensiveness in return. (Also reconsider your perceptions because your husband cannot fall short in *all* things.)

What if beyond his perceived flaw of low sexual desire, your husband's other qualities are good—really good? That's when you need to own your worries, concerns, and fears in this area and ask God to help you bear them. You are responsible for your own insecurities, of course, but God wants to be there for you. He can help you forgive your husband for his resistance to seeking help. You likely feel overwhelmed by the situation, but consider that your husband might feel the same way. It's also likely that he will reveal his fears differently from you and might even attempt to hide them from you.

When in a period of waiting, some wives have discovered new ways to explore and redefine intimacy with their husbands—ways outside direct sexual contact. We narrow our opportunities for playfulness and exploration when intimacy is regarded only as physical. Abounding in goodness, God has given us more intimacy options that we will delve into in the pages to come.

PART FOUR

Where We Go from Here

14

Embracing Healthy Sexuality

HEALTHY SEXUALITY IN MARRIAGE will never match what Hollywood or romance novels portray. Those make-believe storylines intentionally shift reality into fantasy. That's why it's time to stop taking our cues from those sources.

So what *should* healthy sexuality in marriage look like? What does the Bible say about it? Understanding healthy sexuality involves examining where the seeds of passion originate. Yes, our erogenous zones play a role, but passion typically starts in the brain through our senses—touch, taste, sight, smell, and sound. When I ask couples to describe love and sexuality, I hear from them that love is a feeling like butterflies in your stomach, while sexuality is like looking across the room and *knowing* the object of longing and desire. Very seldom do any of them describe love as an action or a choice, and they typically speak of sexuality as little more than "chemistry" or even lust. This leads me to conclude that few couples have a basic understanding of God's design for love and sexuality in marriage.

Yet Jesus modeled love through action and choice, and He demonstrated it with mercy, empathy, and kindness. He also connected with others through our human senses—touch, sight, smell, taste, and sound. Each moment was about *knowing* in the deepest spiritual sense. Jesus knew the hearts of the people. He could essentially see into another person's soul (see Luke 5:22-23).

The rest of us, obviously, can't know what others are thinking. In preparing for this book, I relied on previous research about healthy sexuality, sensuality, and intimacy. After just a few hours, my head was spinning. I finally found the following definition of sexual health from the World Health Organization: "a state of physical, emotional, mental, and social well-being in relation to sexuality. . . . Sexual health requires a positive and respectful approach to sexuality and sexual relationships, as well as the possibility of having pleasurable and safe sexual experiences, free of coercion, discrimination and violence."[1]

Notice for a moment that absolutely nothing spiritual is included in this description. Nothing about how God's design for sexuality was wired into us at Creation. Nothing about *knowing* another intimately. Instead, our modern understanding of sexuality is primarily focused on pleasure—on what one can *get* instead of *give*. There is seldom safety in this space.

What jumps out to me is that Christians are not defining their sexuality or intimacy—the world is. I believe that one reason for the countless struggles and low sexual satisfaction in marriage is that it's difficult for us to truly reveal our souls to another. We protect ourselves and hide more than ever, mostly because we don't feel safe in our sexual experiences.

Michael Sytsma, a cofounder (with Debra Taylor) of Sexual Wholeness Inc., says that the fear of hurt feelings and the fear of conflict—especially when these fears limit communication—can undermine a fulfilling sex life.[2]

In *Sacred Sex*, Tim Alan Gardner describes the spiritual aspect of intimacy as a way for a husband and wife to "touch each other's soul."[3]

Yet fear can easily undermine this soul connection.

One soul-revealing woman in the Bible who didn't let fear undermine her sexuality is the Shulammite woman, the bride of Solomon described in Song of Solomon. Typical cultural or religious stereotypes do not define her. She is not passive, but bold. She is active in pursuing her lover. She is knowledgeable, open, and unafraid to voice her needs (see Song of Solomon 1:2, 1:4, and 5:8).

The Shulammite woman describes her lover through her senses of touch, taste, smell, and sight (Song of Solomon 5:10-16). She feels deeply known, and she knows her lover (Song of Solomon 7:10). This is how Scripture characterizes sex, and it's not an act of *getting* what she feels she deserves.

Throughout the text, she is an active participant in building healthy spiritual, physical, and emotional connections based on the cultural traditions for engagement and marriage at that time in history. She is respectful and dignified. She models initiating, giving, and receiving. None of her words or behaviors are coercive, demanding, shaming, or motivated by fear. There are no rights or obligations here—only mutuality in every aspect of the relationship between her and her lover.

The biblical significance of the Shulammite woman is in helping us better understand healthy sexuality and a woman's special worth in marriage. Her words and actions teach us that God does not expect us to suppress or fear our passions, but to properly embrace them.

AFFECTION AND INTIMACY CONFUSION

Affection and *intimacy* are not necessarily synonymous with *sex*. That statement bears repeating: Affection and intimacy are not synonymous with sex. It's important to reconsider our perceptions and adopt a mindset that no longer conforms to the ways of this world. Based on the current circumstances of your specific marriage situation, this might require a shift in how you view the gift of sex.

A pornography addiction is typically in conflict with experiencing healthy sexual intimacy, such that a husband who was exposed to sexual images during childhood or adolescence via pornography will often have difficulty fostering positive intimacy in marriage. His wife might feel like more of an object than a cherished partner. Early in their marriage, the new and exciting rush of brain chemicals like dopamine might have covered for his lack of ability to bond, but over time the couple will feel less and less connected. The brain chemicals that spark attraction (excited love) are dopamine and adrenaline; the chemicals that foster long-term attachment (quiet love) are oxytocin and vasopressin.[4]

Oxytocin is the love and arousal hormone, and dopamine is the reward and motivation chemical that is linked to addiction. If your brain and body feel fantastic (euphoric), you'll want to experience that sensation more and more. This *reward* view of sex reduces it to a biological transaction. Orgasm, while amazing, becomes the *only* goal.

On the contrary, the state that the Bible describes as *being known* by your spouse reaches beyond mere sexual release and into areas of richness, closeness, and intimacy. I might liken it to the difference between Hershey's chocolate and Godiva chocolate. A Hershey's chocolate bar is a nice, sweet treat, but there is a superior smoothness and creaminess in the more expensive Godiva chocolate because of, at least in part, Godiva's higher concentration of cocoa butter. Others have compared a rich chocolate (dopamine) with a soft, yummy cheese (oxytocin).

There's a sign in my kitchen that reads *Chocolate Makes Life Better*. And so does sweetening intimacy. As someone once pointed out, "The best sex acts aren't sexual at all."[5]

You can characterize intimacy as a *state of being* or compare it to a delicious treat shared between you and your husband. You can experience intimacy by being fully present and visually connected, by listening attentively, and by affirming your spouse with words and actions. I'm amazed at how we easily spent hours and hours talking on the phone, sitting in the park together, or lying on a picnic blanket looking at the stars before we married—yet we can't find five words to say to one another over dinner after just a few years of marriage. The process is backward, yet we're baffled as to why we feel spiritually, emotionally, and physically disconnected.

You want to feel connected to your spouse like you once did? Start over from the beginning. Reengage in the act of intimate conversation outside the bedroom. Begin with curious questions: *How do you feel when we have alone time together? What would you like to do for a fun afternoon? Do you ever have worries about us? How are you feeling about the (health/parenting/financial) concerns we're facing?* (Don't be afraid to share that you have fears too. Make it clear that you're asking these questions so you can understand.) *Do you ever think about how you would like to work through these concerns differently? Is there anything in particular you need from me?*

If you can, have such a conversation in the park, on a boat, or sitting by a fire. Your husband might shrug his shoulders a bit, but his thinking wheels will probably start churning. You might consider touching his hand or his knee or rubbing the back of his neck. Perhaps snuggle up against him or lay your head on his shoulder.

One note of caution here: Do not have this conversation in the bedroom. Most of our sexual encounters in marriage take place in the bedroom, so I encourage you to find a place that feels like neutral ground. That way our sexual memories in the bedroom remain treasured, calm, spiritual, and safe, and the bedroom remains the place where God joins us in cultivating oneness with Him and each other. (Unfortunately, serious sexual discussions in marriage can sometimes lead to increased tensions and hurt feelings. We can't eliminate them completely, but we can try to minimize their likelihood.)

I want you to redefine any unhealthy attitudes about love and intimacy. If mutual sexual release isn't happening in your marriage right now, rest assured that there are new and different ways to still love deeply, to experience intimacy through *knowing*, and to demonstrate affection *while* you continue to seek answers regarding your husband's diminished desire. We'll consider those new and different ways next.

15

Redefining Intimacy

IN ORDER TO ADJUST misguided views about intimacy, it's important to examine two specific interactions in the Bible. Both interactions involve women—one occurs at the beginning of Jesus' ministry and the other at the very end. Each one speaks to the depth of connection we long for deep within our hearts.

The first intimate moment is found in Luke 7:37-38:

And behold, a woman of the city, who was a sinner, when she learned that he was reclining at table in the Pharisee's house, brought an alabaster flask of ointment, and standing behind him at his feet, weeping, she began to wet his feet with her tears and wiped them with the hair of her head and kissed his feet and anointed them with the ointment.

The second intimate moment is found in John 12:1-3:

> Six days before the Passover, Jesus therefore came to
> Bethany, where Lazarus was, whom Jesus had raised from
> the dead. So they gave a dinner for him there. Martha
> served, and Lazarus was one of those reclining with
> him at table. Mary therefore took a pound of expensive
> ointment made from pure nard, and anointed the feet
> of Jesus and wiped his feet with her hair. The house was
> filled with the fragrance of the perfume.

In both instances, a woman took down her hair and used it as a towel. Both women laid their honor and worth at His feet and likely walked away knowing Jesus' love. These were intimate and divine moments that met each woman in her place of need. Absolutely nothing is portrayed as sexual with this celibate and holy man.

These were holy encounters filled with grace, respect, knowing, love, connectedness, humbleness, and sacrifice. But today we operate under a more worldly definition of intimacy. Intimacy now primarily refers to pleasurable interactions rather than interactions that heal the heart, mind, and body.

The women in these passages realize there is a man named Jesus who loves them unconditionally, without demands or strings attached. They recognize that they can have their hearts intimately *known*. Their world changes as they sit at His feet. These scenes from Scripture teach us about intimacy, both with our Lord and Savior and with our husbands.

Intimacy redefined is not complicated. It involves the divine moments in our days when we can sit and talk with Jesus. His presence surrounds us, comforts us, hears us, captures our tears, and loves us when we are confused and discouraged, fearful or sad. The Lord continues to *know* us when our husband falters or his body breaks down.

If you are having one of those days—when nothing in your marriage feels like it's changing for the better—consider the words of Psalm 91:4: "He will cover you with his feathers, and under his wings you will find refuge; his faithfulness will be your shield and rampart" (NIV).

That's why it's important to give up the narrowly focused view of intimacy that defines it as erotic or sexual in nature. Intimacy is vital in friendships, after all, and many couples who transition from the pressures of raising children to the relative quiet of an empty nest find their friendship faltering. Redefining intimacy in your marriage means focusing on connecting with your husband, even when his body can't respond the way you want because of physical or mental illness, medications, or ongoing healing from porn or past abuse.

Can you still create an intimate marriage? I certainly believe it's possible, as long as both of you are willing to consider changes and explore new options. A healthy, growing marriage integrates numerous kinds of intimacy, but this requires intention, attention, and *action*. I recently heard one wife say, "I want an organic marriage." In other words, she wanted it to come naturally, without effort. Sorry, but a strong marriage doesn't just come naturally. Effort is mandatory.

Sex is certainly one aspect of intimacy, but marriage includes many forms of intimacy that are just as important. Intimacy in a thriving marriage can involve almost any form of interaction that brings about intimate connection for both husband and wife. If intercourse never becomes a regular part of a marriage, in what other areas of the relationship can a couple focus on intimacy?

PRAYER: THE SCARY KIND OF INTIMACY

Prayer is that part of intimacy that requires peeling off our emotional plastic wrap in order to access those oh-so-secret places that no one else can get to—the areas that involve vulnerability and sharing how your heart really feels. That includes your relationship with God. (I'll admit right now that my own heart can be a bit dark and moldy at times.)

In speaking with couples and individuals, I can't tell you how many times I've heard, "My relationship with God is private." Yet if you want an intimate marriage, guess what? Keeping your relationship with God a secret from your spouse is not going to work. After all, the healthiness or unhealthiness of this so-called secret relationship usually seeps out somehow, most often through the words that flow from our mouths. But that reality apparently hasn't sunk in, as we have plenty of company in trying to maintain this mindset of secrecy.

After consulting all the Christian marriage resources on my bookshelves, the best estimate I can come up with is that about *8 percent* of Christian couples pray together regularly. (Note that I did not say *daily*.) That number is incredibly sobering, and I suspect that it's only continuing to decrease over time.

Take a moment to ask yourself:

- What are my personal barriers to praying with my spouse?
- What do I fear will happen if we pray together?
- Will prayer create further disconnection or bring us closer together?

Several years ago I wrote an article describing how uncomfortable I was in praying with my husband, and how I looked for any excuse to avoid it.[1] It wasn't until a small group leader encouraged us to give joint prayer a try that I reluctantly decided to dip my toes in the water. (To be honest, I used to accuse my husband of sounding like Shakespeare when he prayed because he knew Latin from attending parochial grade school. Those were definitely not among my more tactful moments as a wife!)

We eventually agreed to write down our prayers during the day and share the highlights at dinner or bedtime. This one simple step toward developing intimacy through prayer changed the trajectory of our marriage and ministry.

My point here is to *start somewhere*. Whether it's sharing notes made on your phone or in a journal, reading a couple's devotional together, or simply telling your husband, "I'd like to share the conversation I had with God today," it's definitely not as scary as you've come to believe. And prayer is incredibly essential during the yucky seasons we endure in marriage, especially when we do not feel like being compassionate or understanding—sometimes for days or weeks at a time.

If you're committed to Jesus Christ being the foundation of your marriage, do not be one of the 92 percent (or more) who neglect praying together regularly. Put in the effort to make it a part of your daily intimacy routine.

AN ATMOSPHERE OF TOUCH

Touch is an aspect of intimacy that might require learning the beauty of affectionate, nonsexual contact by focusing on physical connection that unfolds outside the bedroom. Consider the following question I often ask the seriously dating or engaged couples I work with: If an illness or injury were to take away your physical sex life (intercourse), what do you think would remain in terms of your intimacy?

In many cases, the couples respond with a question of their own: "What do you mean?"

I then elaborate:

- If sickness instead of health shows up sooner rather than later in your marriage, and intercourse is no longer a physical possibility, would your relationship survive?
- Would you remain committed to a future together if it happened tomorrow?
- Could you trust each other to remain faithful?

I pose these grim scenarios with seriously dating and engaged couples for a reason: Unforeseen tragedies and those unexpected moments of "for worse" or "in sickness" *do* surface in marriage. In working with couples for years, I've helped some of them process cancer of the testicles, bladder, colon, uterus, and kidneys. I've encountered couples dealing with multiple sclerosis, lupus, and Lyme disease, as well as automobile, work, and military-related injuries. Some of these maladies occurred within a month of the wedding day.

You never imagined that it might happen to you, yet you now have this book in your hands because of your husband's lack of desire. The pain feels overwhelming, and you don't want to consider what might happen if his desire levels remain low or nonexistent. I believe your marriage can and should survive this, but I am not naive enough to assume that many wives haven't at least considered their options.

WORKING-SIDE-BY-SIDE INTIMACY

In the busy moments of our day, we seldom disconnect from the stress associated with work and family life. Yet your marriage needs those unplugged moments—whether they're spent redecorating a bedroom together or simply hanging out in the garage while one or both of you tinker at some repair.

Consider volunteering together at a local food pantry or helping the elderly in your community take care of their yards. One couple who both love to paint changed their relationship by volunteering with Habitat for Humanity. Your efforts might even help foster other sorts of intimacy. For example, beautifying your backyard with new plants, bird feeders, and a small fountain will result in an outdoor sanctuary for the two of you to enjoy together. No matter what you do, the goal is increased connection and more intimacy.

TIME-ALONE-FOR-US INTIMACY

Just the two of you alone, with no kids, no family, and no friends around, is a gift. It's also vital. During the pandemic, many couples shared the desire to slow down and begin appreciating a less hectic pace. One couple decided that rather than become Netflix junkies, they'd become foreign language experts and spend time learning Spanish and Italian. Another couple decided to start enjoying evening baths together. (Just make sure you have a big enough tub!) Perhaps the best part of such pastimes is that they work even on cold and rainy days.

When outdoor activities are available, gardening, boating, fishing, exploring art fairs, hanging out in the garage, and biking together are all time investments in the two of you. If you don't share a lot of common interests, almost everyone can enjoy a side-by-side walk around the neighborhood or a quick trip to pick up your favorite coffee or other beverage.

Spending time alone together is great, but we still need to be on the lookout for intimacy-stealing distractions. Perhaps the most common of these today is *technoference*, short for "technology-based interference." Technoference disrupts the flow of time and connection in relationships, and the most common version for couples is when one or both spouses spend time together, each one looking at a screen instead of engaging with the other.[2]

Technoference sends a clear message about what we do or do not value most. In research published by *Psychology of Popular Media Culture*, 38 percent of respondents acknowledged sending texts or emails while having a conversation with their partner.[3] Demonstrating inattention sends a clear message of distance and emotional detachment. In 2023, Americans spent an average of 5.4 hours a day on their phones. (Social media accounted for nearly two and a half hours of online time each day.)[4] If we can't go for even small stretches of time without our phones, we're in trouble when it comes to our chances for prioritizing intimate connection with our spouses.

The Gottman Institute learned that couples who spend about six hours a week building their relationship have found what the researchers called a "winning formula." The six hours includes time for partings and reunions; appreciation, admiration, and affection; about two hours for a weekly date night; plus time for a regular check-in or "state of the union" meeting.[5] Yet my experience with couples—especially those who are in the midst of raising children—reflects that they devote barely one hour a week toward keeping intimacy thriving.

AWE-AND-WONDER INTIMACY

When and where do the two of you feel most connected to God? Have you ever discussed this as a couple? Consider exploring music, nature, art, and creativity together. Many feel a closeness to God near the water. The power and majesty of the waves, along with the sounds and smells of the ocean, can be awe-inspiring. So can standing by a small, fast-moving stream in the mountains.

Water isn't a requirement, of course. We also see the glory of creation when watching a roadrunner scoot quickly across a desert landscape or noticing the vegetation's various shapes and colors. Sunrises, sunsets, and sunlight streaming through the clouds after a thunderstorm also lend themselves to awe and wonder.

The word *majesty* speaks to God's greatness, and it is also an invitation to worship Him. Enjoying intimate moments like this together help make Him more prominent in our lives and in our souls. It's better to breathe in His awe and wonder through creation than to inhale even more stress.

Have you and your husband ever experienced a moment quiet enough that you could hear each other breathing while curled up together under a blanket watching the stars? On a recent trip to Arizona, a friend learned about Dark Sky Cities and decided to visit an observatory outside Flagstaff. A Dark Sky City must abide by specific guidelines regarding light pollution.[6] My friend and her husband watched the stars for hours and pointed out constellations to one another for what felt like the entire evening.

In case you haven't gotten the message here, I want you to try something new. Explore moments together in those places where you each feel most connected to God. Since He is eternal, almighty, majestic, and infinite, you shouldn't have to go very far.

If you are in a season of not knowing whether your physical intimacy will improve or remain the same, this type of intimate experience might help move you out of a fearful place. Lean on God to meet both of you right where you are. An awe-and-wonder experience might soften your hearts and ease your minds as you enjoy a different kind of intimacy.

WHEN THERE IS NO INTIMACY

If you've made it this far in the book, I'm guessing there is one type of intimacy that you desperately wish to experience with your husband. All your time, energy, and focus might have brought you to a place of thinking, *It's not fair. I'm horribly frustrated and angry. The sexual connection I wish to have with my husband does not exist at the level I desire.*

First, it is completely understandable to struggle with frustration. Maybe you stomp your feet and cry out to God for missing what you see as a critical aspect of your marriage. That said, I want you to try to expand your focus.

Some of you reading this chapter have probably dealt with zero to little sexual intimacy for a very long time. Some feel punished and even abused. Some have had ups and downs. I want to acknowledge that many times there are no easy solutions; you can only step back and wrestle with God. That wrestling should include directing your frustrations and questions to Him: *I'm dying inside, and my marriage is not getting better in the sex department. Some marriages get to move forward even a little, but mine is stalled out completely. God, what do You wish for me to do with this aspect of my marriage?*

As we've discussed in this chapter, there are numerous ways to explore intimacy and connection with your husband—ways you might have never considered before. Asking God to meet you in your moments of uncertainty can help bring clarity to the complex and challenging seasons in marriage, but we always seem to prefer quick solutions. I wish I could provide them.

I know you probably purchased this book in the hope of getting some quick solutions. It can be frustrating to consider, but sometimes we need to redefine how we view intimacy and the purposes that God might have for us in those times of "wait and see." God is patient with us, and He loves us. I truly believe not only that He is good, but also that He often has something in store for us that we haven't considered. (Not to mention that an attitude of impatience does not reflect well on us or benefit our husbands.)

Take a moment to again consider:

Are you setting up the man in your life for failure?

Comparing your marriage with others or comparing your husband with other men will do that. Viewing your situation through a *fair-or-unfair* filter will do that. Resentments and negative attitudes will do that.

Some wives will move on from here with hope as they begin to understand the reasons their husbands may be wired differently. Some wives will decide to explore intimacy in new and different ways with their husbands, recognizing that desire levels are seldom the same. Some will work through desire differences for a few months and others for years.

Some of you might throw up your hands and say, "I wasted my money. This book provides no easy solutions. I still can't have sex with my husband." I want you to know that I feel your frustration and your hurt. There are options to explore, but it's up to you to decide if sex is the focus of your marriage or if love is. If the physical act of sex is never again a possibility, will you choose to love your husband intimately in new ways, or will you become cold and distant?

16

Rewriting Our Stories

AS WE PRACTICE RESPONDING to a difficult situation in our marriage, how do we look to make our relationship more biblical and mutual in the days to come? Can we embrace a narrative that tells us we are worthy of love and acceptance, even though we can't demand these things from a particular person? Can we accept the sometimes-harsh realities of life, even if our situation is not the one we imagined?

These questions should remind us that our husband is also worthy of being loved and accepted. How do we let go of our resentment toward him and our tendency to justify past behaviors that have contributed to the situation or have failed to improve it? How do we embrace a life of gratitude for what we do have rather than focusing on what we don't?

Is it possible to look for goodness in your husband instead of failure? Can you find some Christlikeness in how he tries to love you? *Seriously, are you telling me I'm supposed to look for that?* Yes, I am. Are you focusing on the thing you can't have right now instead of the many things he lovingly provides and genuinely gives from his heart? I want you to consider how he shows you his love in small ways, the best ways he knows—ways you might seldom notice because your hurting heart and a critical spirit can be your worst enemies.

Don't make your husband the enemy, falling prey to negative emotional patterns and reactions. Unless your husband has turned his back on you and on God, keep in mind that you are really working against medical, mental health, or emotional issues, not each other. *You are not meant to be enemies.* And even if it feels that way right now, God gives us a challenge when He instructs us, "I'm telling you to love your enemies. Let them bring out the best in you, not the worst. When someone gives you a hard time, respond with the supple moves of prayer, for then you are working out of your true selves, your God-created selves" (Matthew 5:44-45, MSG).

A GOOD MAN, A LOVING HEART

Did God give you a decent husband with a loving heart? He might have. I'm guessing that your husband did not choose lower desire on purpose. We've already addressed cruelty, callous treatment, and abuse. But let's try to make an optimistic assumption: God gave you a decent man. Unless he *is* callous or cruel, he's a man who says he loves you. He tells you you're beautiful. He loves your children, family, friends, neighbors, and church community. In other words, maybe the fact that you're reading this right now is God's way of giving you insight into your husband's heart.

There's more.

Is he still the kind of husband who remembers to bring you your favorite coffee? He still knows you like the almond mocha oat milk latte, and he doesn't forget the three pumps of caramel. He apologizes for not giving (or being able to give) you what it feels like you need the most right now. He acknowledges that it hurts. He's still a man who works hard, goes to church with you, and is willing to pray with you. He is still a man who gives from his soul.

Of course, if he's not any of those things, then a physical, sexual relationship is *not* your biggest concern right now. But if he is some or many of those things, then try to embrace those parts of his being.

Here's where you have to look deep inside yourself. Wherever your husband is at mentally or physically, he cannot or doesn't want to give you the thing you want: sexual oneness. Physical unity. Intercourse. As a result, does your heart focus on that aspect and that one aspect alone? Do you have a voice inside that tells you, *I cannot live without this from him?*

Is that really the voice you will listen to?

KEYSHA'S STORY

After seventeen years of marriage, my husband could not keep an erection even with medication. We stopped talking, touching, and going to church. We did not reach out for help, and I was unwilling to accept anything less than intercourse with him. I have many regrets because I chose divorce and never examined the pain it would cause my family. I expected this choice to bring the happiness and sex I deserved, and today I see my decision as selfish and unforgiving. Two years later I married my current husband, and within six months he was diagnosed with prostate cancer.

TALK AND MORE TALK

Have you and your husband taken time outside the bedroom to discuss new ways to experience intimacy? Avoiding uncomfortable discussions with your husband about sex will not change your situation or emotions, and it will likely create further division. Take negative reactions, blame, pressure, or guilt off the table. The essential ingredients of such communication include sharing preferences, likes and dislikes, comfort and discomfort, and what feels safe and unsafe.

How might the conversations shift or tension-filled moments fade if he heard the following words from you?

"Honey, I'm a wife who loves having sex with you. That may be different from what you've heard about most women. There are many myths, lies, and assumptions about men's and women's sexuality. I've learned that I am not weird but normal—and Scripture confirms it. I have let you down in not loving you well when your desire is lower than mine, and I am deeply sorry."

One of you has to start the conversation, and since you're the one reading this book, you get to go first. This moment of vulnerability on your part, your sharing what might have never been shared before, will help prepare you to work together toward new understandings and lovemaking experiences.

> **Be completely humble and gentle; be patient, bearing with one another in love.**
> EPHESIANS 4:2 (NIV)

Now it's time to turn the page to the next chapter of your marriage. This next chapter involves building a new foundation through prayer, with Jesus as the center. Ask the Lord for insight and wisdom into each other's sexual needs and expectations. Remember that *different from before* does not mean loveless, graceless, or compassionless. Taking this next step requires emotional, physical, and spiritual energy, but it is well worth every bit of it.

Even though I've given you a suggestion for how to begin the conversation, this time of exploring sexual needs and expectations together might still feel overwhelming. If that's the case, I'd recommend reading books or listening to podcasts by author Juli Slattery, cofounder of Authentic Intimacy (AuthenticIntimacy.com). I can speak to the excellent quality of resources and godly wisdom that this organization provides for couples. In addition, Sexual Discipleship (SexualDiscipleship.com) is a newer platform created to help train churches and leaders on sexual topics from a gospel-centered mindset.

Here are some incredible insights shared by Juli Slattery regarding the battle raging against healthy sexuality:

> Even godly, committed Christians are far more likely
> to think like the world on sexual issues because they
> have been trained to do so. . . . The church has offered
> sex education while the culture is sexually discipling
> us, forming our opinions and worldview on everything
> sexual. . . . Much of the media, news outlets, and
> educational leaders are aggressive about passing on their
> sexual values to children and adults. You are shunned
> and ridiculed if you express an opinion that differs from
> these values.
>
> From what you observe through entertainment
> media, news outlets, the government, and the educational
> system, is the messaging about sexuality from the world
> clear and consistent? You bet it is![1]

Some churches are ill-equipped or don't have the staff to handle the needs of engaged and married couples. As a result, there is often a lack of experience in teaching gospel-honoring sexuality both inside and outside marriage. Church is essential, and community is deeply needed in the lives of Christ followers, but we are not without messiness and blemishes. After all, we are all a part of the body, and change is often slow or resisted inside both homes—the one where we live each day, and the one we visit on Sundays.

BUT NOTHING HAS CHANGED (YET)!

If your husband is attending counseling with you and taking small steps forward to bridge the desire gap, then this counts as progress. If he's making and keeping doctor appointments, this is progress. If his track record of follow-through is solid, then this is progress.

Is he transparent with you, even when it's not pretty, and is his heart open to accountability where he previously had none? Is there sorrow and remorse and working to keep himself clean and sober, particularly if pornography was a factor? Do you hear shifts and changes in his words and actions? Are you seeing less resentment and blame from him? This is progress. This is change. No matter how small and how slow, it is change nonetheless.

Yet there are also instances in which we take all the right steps, get the best medical advice, attend counseling, and receive treatment, yet it feels like nothing has changed.

But is that really the case? The truth is that moving forward with an open heart *will* change a relationship eventually. But what if our thoughts—our desired outcomes—are stuck in unrealistic expectations that focus on perfection? Remember that sexual desire ebbs and flows throughout every marriage. Yes, you're going through this season with your husband now, but there could be a time in the future when the tables turn and your husband desires sex more than you. If that happens, you'll want him to cherish you, respect you, and remain faithful to you, just as you are cherishing him, respecting him, and remaining faithful to him right now.

And while you didn't sign up for a no-sex marriage in your wedding vows, you did vow to love and cherish your husband even in hard times. As for who goes first in terms of changing? Putting on a stubborn hat won't work, nor will putting on a blame hat. We know by now that it takes two, and you need some wise, godly counsel regarding the next steps in your marriage.

But why am I being asked to love a broken spouse? That's a great question for God. Maybe the broken part involves an equal amount of him and you. A more accurate answer is that the ideal spouse does not exist here on earth, "for we all stumble in many ways" (James 3:2).

In an article titled "How to Appreciate an Imperfect Spouse," author and pastor Gary Thomas uses James 3:2 to describe the situation this way:

> What James is telling us is that if you were to divorce your spouse, interview two hundred "replacement" candidates, put them through a battery of psychological tests, have follow-up interviews conducted by your closest friends, spent three years dating the most compatible ones, and then spent another forty days praying and fasting about which one to choose, you'd still end up with a spouse who disappoints you, hurts you, frustrates you, and stumbles in many ways. The word "all" means there are no exceptions.[2]

WHAT IF HE'S UNWILLING TO TAKE ANY STEPS?

Some husbands enter marriage unable to maintain an erection. The result is that they often retreat into a full emotional, physical, and/or spiritual shutdown. Nothing the wife tries will motivate him to even address the situation. I usually hear comments like these: "If he'd just try a little. If he'd just talk to me. If he'd just try to understand how I feel. If he'd just . . ."

It bears repeating: When one spouse continually pushes the other to take action, or even just to talk, it's not unusual for the spouse who feels pressured to retreat instead. Even when the first spouse's intentions are good, the more he or she pushes, the other spouse retreats more and more, to the point of shutting down emotionally.

In some cases the shutdown is complete and total, permeating every area of married life, including talking, sharing, learning, and even simply respecting. Interactions become devoid of any emotion, including anger. This is what *indifference* looks like. As we previously discussed, indifference can be incredibly toxic and potentially abusive within a marriage, particularly when a husband refuses to seek any outside help—like when he gives up on seeking positive change or a loving connection. Yet there are also instances when a wife might need to ease up for a while in order to find a healthy path forward.

We cannot and should not judge or admonish a wife who has had to endure living with indifference, and perhaps we shouldn't judge a husband whose wife keeps pushing long after it becomes clear that her efforts aren't achieving the desired outcome. Sadly, I've seen many husbands shift into callous treatment, thereby eliminating the possibility of change and healing. And of course any emotionally abusive or manipulative behavior is never acceptable and is the ultimate impediment to meaningful progress.

If you have a spouse with a hardened heart, I make a plea to you: Do not allow your own heart to harden too. Even if we only flirt with such behavior, we run the risk of becoming someone we no longer recognize.

17

No Longer Alone

YOU MIGHT REACH THE END of this journey and discover the sexual life you've always hoped for with your husband. You might reach the end of this journey and find that things have improved—perhaps not in a romance-novel sort of way, but hopefully you've found contentment. You might find that your sex life has changed—but not the way you were hoping for. Or, sadly, you might find that things have stayed the same or even gotten worse. You began the journey seeking answers, yet I've said time and again that there are no easy ones.

No matter which scenario best describes your individual situation, I hope you discovered the universal response that applies in every single instance: It's time to lay down fear, rejection, and isolation and embrace the truth that no matter what happens—or doesn't happen—in the bedroom, we can trust God.

We can embrace the gift God has provided us in our husband. There's much more than sexual desire to the man God gave you to love. You don't want to view him as a one-dimensional, merely sexual being. His value is based on so much more than his ability to perform. You can also know and embrace that whatever happens in the bedroom, you are a woman of worth and beauty—just the way you are.

> God gave us a spirit not of fear but of power and love and self-control.
>
> 2 TIMOTHY 1:7

God sees and hears your heartache, and He's near to the brokenhearted (see Psalm 34:18). In other words, you don't have to carry this burden alone. He will help you. Not only that, but you *are* allowed to talk about your struggles with safe and trustworthy individuals. You can do so, carefully and discreetly, outside the bedroom and within the walls of the church. And you can do so while remaining authentic to who you are.

You don't have to feel shame or believe you are responsible for everything that feels sexually broken in your marriage. (Likewise, should your husband bear all the responsibility? It's a question you need to consider.) Yet by allowing God and others to provide love, comfort, and understanding, you can find peace in your life and marriage. You can receive reassurance from other women who'll walk beside you—and someday you might likewise provide comfort to other women who also struggle with desire discrepancy in marriage.

IS GOD ASKING TOO MUCH?

Why is God asking me to carry this burden in my marriage? If my husband has a mental or medical condition, can I be doing more to help him with his burden? What if God wants me to shift my focus off myself?

Psalm 55:22 tells you to "pile your troubles on GOD's shoulders—he'll carry your load, he'll help you out. He'll never let good people topple into ruin" (MSG).

How God is working on and through your husband is between the two of them. (That's probably another concept that you don't want to hear.) Remain focused on your own heart, and allow God to work in your husband's.

Perhaps God is saying, *Stop trying so hard to fix things and attempting to redesign your husband. Let Me do My work in him. Watch, wait, and listen patiently.*

This is your opportunity to embrace the concept of *abiding*. To abide means to make a choice to keep pressing on, accepting, bearing with, remaining, dwelling, staying the course, and persevering, among other things. Throughout Scripture, numerous promises tell us that we are not alone—that God abides with His people.

In his article "Braving Loneliness," clinical psychologist and author Kelly Flanagan writes, "When someone abides with you, it means they are choosing to be with you, before all others. It implies that they will stay with you through whatever comes, that they will sing with you on this boat called companionship during the terrible storms raging on the seas of life. Abiding doesn't stop the storm, but it changes the hearts and spirits of those who choose to sail together."[1]

That description somewhat sounds like the vows you made when you got married, don't you think? Your husband needs you to persevere with him. He needs to know that he is not alone in dealing with the struggles he's facing. Sexual desire will ebb and flow—and feelings will inevitably change—throughout the course of a marriage. But true love abides.

A Message to Husbands

YOU ARE PROBABLY reading this because someone invited you to do so, most likely your spouse. How do I know? Because this is primarily a book for women. And if the woman in your life asked you to read this section of the book—a book about *sexual desire differences*—then it's likely because she wants you to hear the perspective of a husband.

That's me. I'm the author's husband. And here is my perspective.

- I'll state the obvious first: Since your wife is reading this book, it's likely that she has a higher desire level than you. This book is her way of inviting you into a conversation. You need to know that desire differences occur in every marriage, and it's okay if your desire level is less than hers. In fact, it's not that unusual.

- I'm guessing that asking you to read this was uncomfortable and maybe even a bit risky for her. It took courage. So thank her for caring about you and your marriage. Listen to her. Be open and honest. You have a wife who loves you and wants a great relationship. Do everything in your power to not withdraw from her.

- She's hoping for a response from you after you read this. My advice: Try to talk to her before she asks.

- You might already be aware of the problem. You might even know what the cause is.

- Is pornography and self-gratification a factor? Pornography can change the way your brain reacts to arousal, making you less likely to feel aroused by your wife. If porn is involved, a good first step might be sharing this concern with a trained and trusted church leader, licensed counselor, Christian sex therapist, or sexual-addiction specialist. (Additional resources and counselor referrals are available by calling Focus on the Family at 1-855-771-4357 or by visiting **ChristianCounselorsNetwork.com**. For specific resources dealing with pornography, visit **FocusOnTheFamily.com /Pornography**.) As hard as it might be to admit the issue, you will definitely have better success breaking the habit if you do. And definitely *don't* make your wife your accountability partner. There are lots of resources available for men who deal with this issue, but if you're not sure where to begin, you can learn more at Marriagetrac.com.

- Is something going on with you physically? Do you struggle with low energy? Erectile dysfunction (ED)? Stress? Depression? Maybe it has to do with medication you are—or aren't—taking. No matter the cause, get the help you need. Make an appointment with a physician or a trained mental health therapist.

Finally, here are a few guy tips—man-to-man advice from me to you:

- Do not pull away from your wife physically, emotionally, or spiritually.
- Try to understand her needs. Empathize with her feelings. Listen and be patient.
- Never give her the silent treatment.
- Accept her help and take the feasible steps necessary to maximize the physical, emotional, and spiritual health of your relationship. Share with each other your goals and the steps you're taking.
- Love your wife. Every day, ask yourself, "What can I do to love her better?" Draw close to her. Every day, tell her she's beautiful. Intimacy is about a lot more than sex.
- Initiate prayer with your wife. Even better, make praying together a part of your routine.
- Once again, listen to her. Give her your full attention when she's speaking. (No looking at the TV, your tablet, or your phone!)

Last but not least, ask the Lord to help both of you. You're in this together, and I wish you all the success in the world.

Jim Mueller

Resources

Mental and Physical Health

DEPRESSION

Ongoing indicators of depressive symptoms include the following:

- Emotional: irritability and anger, feelings of worthlessness or inappropriately placed guilt, lack of pleasure in most activities, pessimism or emptiness
- Physical: lower testosterone levels, fatigue, lack of energy, erectile and other sexual dysfunction, anxiety, restlessness, significant weight loss or weight gain, insomnia or sleeping too much
- Cognitive: difficulty concentrating, memory lapses, obsessive-compulsive thoughts, suicidal thoughts
- Behavioral: increased alcohol consumption or use of other addictive substances, uncharacteristic risky behaviors[1]

According to a poll of 21,000 American men by researchers at the National Center for Health Statistics (NCHS), nearly one in ten men reported experiencing some form of depression or anxiety, but fewer than half sought treatment.[2] In other words, men are typically less likely than women to seek help with depression, substance abuse, and stressful life events in general.

According to Mental Health America, this is due to

- social stereotypes that suggest "real men" don't need therapy,
- a general reluctance to talk about their problems, and
- a tendency among men to downplay their symptoms.[3]

According to a National Health Interview Survey, of the nearly 10 percent of men in the US who experience anxiety or depression on a daily basis, only one in three takes medication because of those feelings, while one in four actually speaks with a mental health professional.[4] Much of the reluctance among men to seek treatment stems from societal expectations and traditional gender roles, which can compel men to think they must

- be the primary income earners in their families,
- behave in traditionally masculine ways, such as showing strength and extreme self-control,
- depend on themselves and avoid relying on others, and
- keep their emotions hidden.[5]

You and your husband might have concerns about unusual and potentially alarming symptoms. Relying on a Google search will likely leave you either confused or convinced that something is there that is not there. Instead, please consult with a physician, psychologist, psychiatrist, or other licensed therapist. In addition to providing an accurate assessment, that person can also assist in determining the diagnostic criteria required by insurance carriers.[6]

ANXIETY

The National Institute of Mental Health defines generalized anxiety disorder as excessive worry or anxiety about normal daily life, occurring more days than not, for a period of six months or more.[7] The following list doesn't include every symptom of anxiety, yet it provides enough information to help you understand the basics:

- Edginess or restlessness
- Becoming easily tired or being more fatigued than usual
- Impaired concentration; feeling as though one's mind has gone blank
- Irritability (which may or may not be observable to others)
- Increased muscle aches or soreness; stomachaches
- Difficulty sleeping (trouble falling asleep or staying asleep, restlessness at night, or unsatisfying sleep)[8]

OTHER CONDITIONS

Additional conditions that are important to discuss with a medical professional include a significant drop in testosterone and other age-related hormone changes, hypoactive sexual interest/arousal disorder, and hypogonadism (which occurs during fetal development or is due to infection or injury).

According to the *Journal of Global Health*, the United States lags behind some other countries in the area of men's health care:

Only four countries—Australia, Brazil, Iran, and Ireland—have developed national men's health policies. In most other countries, men's health is not recognized as an issue of concern by governments or health providers.[9]

Pornography and Sex Addiction

Many pornography or sex addiction programs are not covered by health insurance programs, but some of them do offer financial assistance. The truth is that the American psychiatric community hasn't reached any sort of consensus in defining a treatment protocol for compulsive sexual behaviors. Neither have they established a point at which these behaviors become troublesome to the individual seeking help. According to the Mayo Clinic, because compulsive sexual behavior doesn't have its own diagnostic category in the DSM-5, it may be diagnosed as a subcategory of another mental health condition, such as an impulse control disorder or a behavioral addiction.[10]

These issues are all the more reason to ask detailed questions about what diagnoses your insurance provider will or will not cover.

I believe some changes are forthcoming with the American Psychiatric Association, but the organization remains painfully slow on this issue, and American insurance providers are even further behind. Perhaps things will begin to move forward since the World Health Organization added compulsive sexual behavior disorder (CSBD) to the International Statistical Classification of Diseases and Related Health Problems in January 2022. CSBD is an impulse disorder "characterized by a persistent pattern of failure to control intense, repetitive sexual impulses or urges resulting in repetitive sexual behavior."[11]

If you are in need of assistance in this area, there are many good programs across the country. One Christian program is Bethesda Workshops (BethesdaWorkshops.org) in Nashville, Tennessee. This program supports a husband and wife not only individually but also as a couple. Other leading programs are Faithful & True (FaithfulAndTrue.com), Pure Desire Ministries (PureDesire.org), Be Broken Ministries (BeBroken.com), and the

HopeQuest Ministry Group (HopeQuestGroup.org). You can discover additional resources by visiting **FocusOnTheFamily.com /Pornography** or by calling 1-855-771-4357.

Many churches across the country also have pornography-related support groups for men and their wives. When in doubt, try to find a Christian therapist with training as a certified sex addiction therapist (CSAT). Focus on the Family maintains a national list of qualified Christian counselors, many of whom specialize in these issues. Learn more by visiting **FocusOnTheFamily.com /GetHelp**.

Finally, Fight the New Drug (FightTheNewDrug.org) is a secular nonprofit agency that launched in 2009 with a campaign that proclaimed *Porn Kills Love*, and several celebrities have endorsed the campaign.[12] Fight the New Drug uses science, facts, and personal stories to educate the public that porn usage leads to poorer-quality relationships and harms the emotional health of a user.

About the Author

SHERI MUELLER is a licensed clinical professional counselor (LCPC) who specializes in working with individuals, premarital couples, and married couples to help them gain insight and hope toward building and maintaining healthy relationships. Sheri is also the cofounder (along with her husband, Jim) of Growthtrac Ministries, which includes a marriage-specific arm called Marriagetrac. Marriagetrac.com is the ministry's online media platform, where married couples can find creative and current articles and expert advice.

Sheri is also certified as a facilitator and trainer for Prepare/ Enrich, a customized couple-assessment tool that identifies a couple's strengths and potential areas for growth. She and her husband are the coauthors of *Restoring What's Been Lost: Six Steps to Claiming Victory over Porn Addiction*, and Sheri has contributed numerous articles and other content to Marriagetrac.com.

In addition to her counseling and mentoring work, Sheri has served as an adjunct professor in the area of individual and group interventions. Sheri earned her bachelor's degree in human services from Judson University and a master's degree in professional counseling from Olivet Nazarene University. Sheri and Jim are high school sweethearts who have been married for more than forty years and have two daughters and five grandchildren, as well as a female rescue kitty named Cassie. They make their home in the suburbs of Chicago.

Notes

PART ONE | THE PROBLEM:
"WHY AM I ALWAYS THE ONE TO BLAME?"

CHAPTER 1 | HE WON'T HAVE SEX WITH ME

1. Alan Mozes, "Who's Got the Strongest Sex Drive, Men or Women?," HealthDay, October 26, 2022, https://consumer.healthday.com/sex-drive -2658474704.html. See also "Q&A: Is It Possible for the Woman to Be the Higher Drive Partner?," Authentic Intimacy, August 9, 2023, YouTube video, 2:03, https://www.youtube.com/watch?v=Iz9BrHUlnl0.

2. Doug Cartwright, "25 Popular Brené Brown Quotes on Empathy, Shame, and Trust," The Daily Shifts, April 2, 2021, https://www.thedailyshifts .com/blog/25-popular-brene-brown-quotes-on-empathy-shame-and-trust.

CHAPTER 2 | MY HUSBAND DOESN'T GET IT

1. Philip Yancey, *Rumors of Another World: What on Earth Are We Missing?* (Grand Rapids, MI: Zondervan, 2003), 75–76.

CHAPTER 3 | I MUST BE THE PROBLEM

1. Ian Kerner, *So Tell Me about the Last Time You Had Sex: Laying Bare and Learning to Repair Our Love Lives* (New York: Grand Central Publishing, 2021), 104. Graphic reproduced with permission.

2. Kerner, *So Tell Me about the Last Time*, 104.

3. Pastor Rick Warren, "What gives me the most hope every day is God's Grace; Knowing that His Grace is going to give me the strength for whatever I face, knowing that nothing is a surprise to God," Facebook, October 29, 2015, https://www.facebook.com/pastorrickwarren/posts /what-gives-me-the-most-hope-every-day-is-gods-grace-knowing-that-his -grace-is-go/10153665628940903.

CHAPTER 4 | THE LIES AND ASSUMPTIONS WE BELIEVE

1. Juli Slattery, *Rethinking Sexuality: God's Design and Why It Matters* (Colorado Springs, CO: Multnomah, 2018), 8.
2. David J. A. Clines, *Interested Parties: The Ideology of Writers and Readers of the Hebrew Bible* (Sheffield, UK: Sheffield Academic, 1995), 214.
3. Julia T. Wood, *Gendered Lives: Communication, Gender, and Culture*, 10th ed. (Belmont, CA: Wadsworth, 1994), 81.
4. Alexia Severson, "Testosterone Levels by Age," Healthline, accessed December 1, 2021, https://www.healthline.com/health/low-testosterone /testosterone-levels-by-age.
5. Randi Hutter Epstein, "The Highs and Lows of Testosterone," *New York Times*, March 27, 2018, https://www.nytimes.com/2018/03/27/well/live /testosterone-supplements-low-t-treatment-libido.html.
6. Kingston Rajiah, Sajesh K. Veettil, Suresh Kumar, and Elizabeth M. Mathew, "Psychological Impotence: Psychological Erectile Dysfunction and Erectile Dysfunction Causes, Diagnostic Methods and Management Options," *Scientific Research and Essays* 7, no. 4 (January 2012), https:// www.researchgate.net/publication/233982369_Psychological_impotence _Psychological_erectile_dysfunction_and_erectile_dysfunction_causes _diagnostic_methods_and_management_options.
7. Arti Patel, "'Dead Bedroom': Stress and Other Factors Ruining Your Sex Life," *Global News*, August 26, 2019, https://globalnews.ca/news/5814296 /factors-ruin-sex-life.
8. Sarah Hunter Murray, *Not Always in the Mood: The New Science of Men, Sex, and Relationships* (Lanham, MD: Rowman and Littlefield, 2019), 24.
9. Murray, *Not Always in the Mood*, 166.
10. Often attributed to Ralph Waldo Emerson. See AZ Quotes, https://www .azquotes.com/quote/89243.
11. Clines, *Interested Parties*, 226.

PART TWO | THE REAL CULPRITS

CHAPTER 5 | HE'S DEALING WITH PHYSICAL, MENTAL, OR NEURODIVERSITY ISSUES

1. American Psychological Association, *Stress in America 2020: A National Mental Health Crisis*, accessed June 12, 2022, https://www.apa.org/news /press/releases/stress/2020/sia-mental-health-crisis.pdf.
2. Sarah H. Murray, Robin R. Milhausen, Cynthia A. Graham, and Leon Kuczynski, "A Qualitative Exploration of Factors That Affect Sexual Desire among Men Aged 30 to 65 in Long-Term Relationships," *Journal of Sex Research* 54, no. 3 (2017): 319–30, http://dx.doi.org/10.1080/00224499 .2016.1168352.

3. "Sexual Dysfunction," Cleveland Clinic, https://my.clevelandclinic
   .org/health/diseases/9121-sexual-dysfunction.
4. Jenna Fletcher, "What Are the Symptoms of Low Testosterone, and
   How to Increase It," Medical News Today, January 26, 2022, https://
   www.medicalnewstoday.com/articles/322647#in-males.
5. "Hypothyroidism (Underactive Thyroid)," Mayo Clinic, https://www
   .mayoclinic.org/diseases-conditions/hypothyroidism/symptoms-causes
   /syc-20350284.
6. William Cole, "Struggling with Low Sex Drive? These 12 Things
   Could Be to Blame," mindbodygreen, November 29, 2020, https://
   www.mindbodygreen.com/articles/reasons-behind-low-sex-drive.
7. "Neurodiversity in the Workplace/Statistics/Update 2023," My Disability
   Jobs, April 12, 2023, https://mydisabilityjobs.com/statistics/neurodiversity
   -in-the-workplace.
8. Joseph Harper, "Too Many Men Ignore Their Depression, Phobias,
   Other Mental Health Issues," *Washington Post*, July 3, 2021, https://
   www.washingtonpost.com/health/mental-health-men/2021/07/02
   /9a199734-d5e5-11eb-ae54-515e2f63d37d_story.html.

CHAPTER 6 | HE'S MEETING HIS NEEDS ELSEWHERE

1. Amanda L. Giordano, "What to Know about Adolescent Pornography
   Exposure," *Psychology Today*, February 27, 2022, https://www
   .psychologytoday.com/us/blog/understanding-addiction/202202
   /what-know-about-adolescent-pornography-exposure.
2. Sam Black, "The Holiday Reality of Peer-to-Peer Porn Exposure," Covenant
   Eyes, updated April 1, 2022, https://www.covenanteyes.com/2019/12/09
   /peer-exposure-porn.
3. Małgorzata Wordecha, Mateusz Wilk, Ewelina Kowalewska, Maciej Skorko,
   Adam Łapiński, and Mateusz Gola, "'Pornographic Binges' as a Key
   Characteristic of Males Seeking Treatment for Compulsive Sexual Behaviors:
   Qualitative and Quantitative 10-Week-Long Diary Assessment," *Journal of
   Behavioral Addictions* 7, no. 2 (June 2018): 438, https://doi.org/10.1556
   /2006.7.2018.33.
4. Justin J. Lehmiller, "The Sexual Secrets Men and Women Hide from Their
   Partners," *Psychology Today*, July 17, 2021, https://www.psychologytoday
   .com/us/blog/the-myths-sex/202107/the-sexual-secrets-men-and-women
   -hide-their-partners. See also Keely Fox, Alexandria M. Ashley, Lacey J.
   Ritter, Tara Martin, and David Knox, "Gender Differences in Sex Secret
   Disclosure to a Romantic Partner," *Sexuality & Culture* 26, no. 1 (February
   2022): 96–115, https://doi.org/10.1007/s12119-021-09880-3.
5. Andrew J. Bauman, "A Pornographic Style of Relating," *Andrew J Bauman*
   (blog), October 1, 2016, https://andrewjbauman.com/a-pornographic
   -style-of-relating.

6. Andrew J. Bauman, *The Sexually Healthy Man: Essays on Spirituality, Sexuality and Restoration* (self-pub., 2021). Used by permission.

7. Sheri Mueller and Jim Mueller, *Restoring What's Been Lost: Six Steps to Claiming Victory over Porn Addiction* (Growthtrac Ministries: 2019).

8. Henry Cloud and John Townsend, *Boundaries in Marriage: Understanding the Choices That Make or Break Loving Relationships* (Grand Rapids, MI: Zondervan, 1999), 107.

9. Tracey Mitchell, *Becoming Brave: How to Think Big, Dream Wildly, and Live Fear-Free* (Nashville: Emanate, 2018), 5.

10. Mueller and Mueller, *Restoring What's Been Lost.*

11. "Most Popular Websites Worldwide as of November 2022, by Total Visits," Statista, January 2023, https://www.statista.com/statistics/1201880/most -visited-websites-worldwide.

12. Barna Group and Josh McDowell Ministry, *The Porn Phenomenon: The Impact of Pornography in the Digital Age* (Ventura, CA: Barna Group, 2016), 80, 109.

13. Mitzi Perdue, "Pornography: The Public Health Crisis of the Digital Age," *Psychology Today*, April 15, 2021, https://www.psychologytoday.com/us /blog/end-human-trafficking/202104/pornography-the-public-health -crisis-the-digital-age.

CHAPTER 7 | HE STRUGGLES WITH INSECURITIES TOO

1. Sarah K. Murnen and Bryan T. Karazsia, "A Review of Research on Men's Body Image and Drive for Muscularity," in *The Psychology of Men and Masculinities*, ed. Ronald F. Levant and Y. Joel Wong (American Psychological Association, 2017), 229–57, https://doi.org/10.1037 /0000023-009.

2. Viren Swami, "Body Image Issues Affect Close to 40% of Men—but Many Don't Get the Support They Need," The Conversation, March 21, 2022, https://theconversation.com/body-image-issues-affect-close-to-40-of-men -but-many-dont-get-the-support-they-need-179046.

CHAPTER 8 | HE HAS BEEN VICTIMIZED

1. "5 Facts about Child on Child Sexual Abuse (COCSA)," Saprea, accessed July 6, 2022, https://saprea.org/blog/child-on-child-sexual-abuse.

2. "Children and Teens: Statistics," Rape, Abuse and Incest National Network (RAINN), accessed July 4, 2022, https://www.rainn.org/statistics/children -and-teens.

3. "The 1 in 6 Statistic," 1in6, accessed July 4, 2022, https://1in6.org/statistic.

4. Richard B. Gartner, "Sexually Abused Boys, and the Men They Become," *Psychology Today*, January 30, 2011, https://www.psychologytoday.com/us /blog/psychoanalysis-30/201101/sexually-abused-boys-and-the-men-they -become.

5. Greg Smalley, "How to Help Your Husband Who Was Sexually Abused as a Child," Focus on the Family, January 15, 2019, https://www .focusonthefamily.com/marriage/how-to-help-your-husband-who-was -sexually-abused-as-a-child.

6. "Sexual Assault of Men and Boys," Rape, Abuse and Incest National Network (RAINN), https://www.rainn.org/articles/sexual-assault-men -and-boys.

CHAPTER 9 | HIS INTERESTS ARE WITH SOMEONE ELSE

1. "The Spectrum," The Trevor Project, https://www.thetrevorproject.org/wp -content/uploads/2017/09/Spectrum-B.pdf.

2. Mere Abrams and Sian Ferguson, "68 Terms That Describe Gender Identity and Expression," Healthline, February 9, 2022, https://www .healthline.com/health/different-genders.

3. Amy Tracy, "My Spouse Struggles with Homosexuality," Focus on the Family, January 1, 2007, https://www.focusonthefamily.com/marriage /my-spouse-struggles-with-homosexuality.

4. Rachel Paula Abrahamson, "Divorced Couple Shares Inspiring Journey after Husband Comes Out as Gay," *Today*, September 13, 2021, https:// www.today.com/parents/couple-who-divorced-after-husband-came-out -gay-open-t230796.

5. Diane Herbst, "Divorced Couple Are Committed to Family after He Comes Out as Gay: 'Our Love Is Different Now,'" *People*, August 12, 2021, https://people.com/human-interest/divorced-couple-remain-committed -family-after-his-coming-out-journey.

6. Joann Condie and Geremy Keeton, *Aftershock: Overcoming His Secret Life with Pornography: A Plan for Recovery* (Colorado Springs, CO: Focus on the Family, 2020).

7. Margaret Feinberg, "7 Ways to Boost Your Mood Today," Margaret Feinberg's official website, https://margaretfeinberg.com/7-ways-boost -mood-today.

8. Erin Smalley, "Why and How to Pursue a Healing Separation," Focus on the Family, December 31, 2020, https://www.focusonthefamily.com/marriage /why-and-how-to-pursue-a-healing-separation.

CHAPTER 10 | HE WITHHOLDS SEX INTENTIONALLY

1. "Understand Relationship Abuse: We're All Affected by the Issue of Domestic Violence," National Domestic Violence Hotline, https:// www.thehotline.org/identify-abuse/understand-relationship-abuse.

2. Leslie Vernick, "Is Marital Indifference Emotionally Abusive?," American Association of Christian Counselors, June 29, 2012, https:// christiancounseling.com/blog/uncategorized/is-marital-indifference -emotionally-abusive.

3. Ellie Lisitsa, "The Four Horsemen: Stonewalling," The Gottman Institute, https://www.gottman.com/blog/the-four-horsemen-stonewalling.

4. Erin Smalley, "Why and How to Pursue a Healing Separation," Focus on the Family, December 31, 2020, https://www.focusonthefamily.com/marriage/why-and-how-to-pursue-a-healing-separation.

CHAPTER 11 | HE DOESN'T LIVE UP TO MY EXPECTATIONS

1. Henry Cloud, "Don't Be the 'Good' Spouse," Boundaries, July 25, 2022, https://www.boundaries.me/blog/don-t-be-the-good-spouse.

2. Tim Alan Gardner, *Sacred Sex: A Spiritual Celebration of Oneness in Marriage* (Colorado Springs, CO: WaterBrook, 2002), 97.

3. Linda Dillow and Lorraine Pintus, *Intimate Issues: 21 Questions Christian Women Ask about Sex* (Colorado Springs, CO: WaterBrook, 1999), 222.

4. Sarah Hunter Murray, *Not Always in the Mood: The New Science of Men, Sex, and Relationships* (Lanham, MD: Rowman and Littlefield, 2019), 171.

PART THREE | SOLUTIONS

CHAPTER 12 | WHAT DIDN'T WORK BEFORE SURELY WON'T WORK AGAIN

1. Les Parrott and Leslie Parrott, "3 Ways to Reignite Your Sex Life for More Intimacy and Fun," SYMBIS Assessment, September 29, 2021, https://www.symbis.com/blog/3-ways-to-reignite-your-sex-life-for-more-intimacy-and-fun.

2. Jenna Fletcher, "How Does Age Affect Erectile Dysfunction?," Medical News Today, updated April 28, 2023, https://www.medicalnewstoday.com/articles/316215.

PART FOUR | WHERE WE GO FROM HERE

CHAPTER 14 | EMBRACING HEALTHY SEXUALITY

1. "Defining Sexual Health: Report of a Technical Consultation on Sexual Health," World Health Organization, January 2002, https://www.cesas.lu/perch/resources/whodefiningsexualhealth.pdf.

2. Ginger Kolbaba, "5 Things Experts Wish You Knew about Healthy Sex in Marriage," Focus on the Family, January 24, 2020, https://www.focusonthefamily.com/marriage/5-things-experts-wish-you-knew-about-healthy-sex-in-marriage.

3. Tim Alan Gardner, *Sacred Sex: A Spiritual Celebration of Oneness in Marriage* (Colorado Springs, CO: WaterBrook, 2002), 5.

4. Information in this paragraph is based on correspondence with Dr. Clifford and Joyce Penner, sex educators and authors of *The Gift of Sex, Restoring the Pleasure, Counseling for Sexual Disorders*, and other popular books on sexuality from a Christian perspective.

5. Ginger Kolbaba, "5 Things Experts Wish You Knew."

CHAPTER 15 | REDEFINING INTIMACY

1. Sheri Mueller, "Simple Words," *Marriage Partnership*, https://www .todayschristianwoman.com/articles/2008/september/23.56.html.
2. Suzanne Degges-White, "Is Technoference Damaging Your Relationships?," *Psychology Today*, March 30, 2022, https://www.psychologytoday.com/us /blog/lifetime-connections/202203/is-technoference-damaging-your -relationships.
3. Sarah M. Coyne and Brandon T. McDaniel, "'Technoference': The Interference of Technology in Couple Relationships and Implications for Women's Personal and Relational Well-Being," *Psychology of Popular Media Culture* 5, no. 1 (January 2016): 85–98, https://doi.org/10.1037 /ppm0000065.
4. Harsha Kiran, "How Much Time Does the Average American Spend on Their Phone in 2023?," Techjury, updated July 27, 2023, https://techjury .net/blog/how-much-time-does-the-average-american-spend-on-their -phone.
5. Kyle Benson, "6 Hours a Week to a Better Relationship," The Gottman Institute, https://www.gottman.com/blog/6-hours-a-week-to-a-better -relationship.
6. "International Dark Sky Places," DarkSky International, https://darksky .org/what-we-do/international-dark-sky-places.

CHAPTER 16 | REWRITING OUR STORIES

1. Juli Slattery, "Sexual Discipleship®: What Is It, and Why Is It Important?," Authentic Intimacy, April 28, 2021, https://www.authenticintimacy .com/resources/2641/the-importance-of-sexual-discipleship.
2. Gary Thomas, "How to Appreciate an Imperfect Spouse," Billy Graham Evangelistic Association, February 12, 2021, https://billygraham.org/story /how-to-appreciate-an-imperfect-spouse.

CHAPTER 17 | NO LONGER ALONE

1. Kelly Flanagan, "Braving Loneliness," adapted from Kelly Flanagan, *True Companions: A Book for Everyone about the Relationships That See Us Through* (Downers Grove, IL: InterVarsity Press, 2021), https://www.marriagetrac .com/braving-lonliness.

RESOURCES

1. Jayne Leonard, "Men's Mental Health: What You Need to Know," Medical News Today, May 31, 2023, https://www.medicalnewstoday.com/articles /mens-mental-health#men-and-mental-health.
2. Stephen Feller, "CDC: Many Men with Depression, Anxiety Untreated,"

United Press International, June 12, 2015, https://www.upi.com/Health
_News/2015/06/12/CDC-Many-men-with-depression-anxiety-untreated
/7341434139241.

3. "5 Minute Guide to Men's Mental Health," Mental Health America,
   https://www.mhanational.org/infographic-mental-health-men.

4. "By the Numbers: Men and Depression," American Psychological Association,
   December 2015, https://www.apa.org/monitor/2015/12/numbers.

5. Leonard, "Men's Mental Health."

6. American Psychiatric Association, *Diagnostic and Statistical Manual of
   Mental Disorders*, 5th ed. (Arlington, VA: American Psychiatric Publishing,
   2013).

7. "Generalized Anxiety Disorder," National Institute of Mental Health,
   https://www.nimh.nih.gov/health/statistics/generalized-anxiety-disorder.

8. "Anxiety Disorders," National Institute of Mental Health, https://www.nimh
   .nih.gov/health/topics/anxiety-disorders.

9. Peter Baker and Tim Shand, "Men's Health: Time for a New Approach
   to Policy and Practice?," *Journal of Global Health* 7, no. 1 (June 2017),
   https://doi.org/10.7189/jogh.07.010306.

10. "Compulsive Sexual Behavior," Mayo Clinic, https://www.mayoclinic
    .org/diseases-conditions/compulsive-sexual-behavior/diagnosis-treatment
    /drc-20360453.

11. Renae Powers, "World Health Organization Confirms Compulsive
    Sexual Behavior Disorder to Be in ICD-11," National Center on Sexual
    Exploitation, June 26, 2019, https://endsexualexploitation.org/articles
    /world-health-organization-confirms-compulsive-sexual-behavior-disorder
    -to-be-in-icd-11.

12. Patty Knap, "Celebrities Sound the Alarm about the Ruin of Pornography,"
    National Catholic Register, February 27, 2016, https://www.ncregister
    .com/blog/celebrities-sound-the-alarm-about-the-ruin-of-pornography.

Make Your Marriage Feel Brand-New

Longing for deeper connection in your marriage? Refresh your relationship at a Marriage Getaway.

Enjoy restful time together as you learn new communication tools from our certified Christian counselors. Growing closer together starts here.

LEARN MORE:
FocusOnTheFamily.com/**Getaway**

Is our marriage over?

It doesn't have to be.

Whatever you're going through—infidelity, intimacy issues, communication breakdowns, etc.—you and your spouse can get started on a path toward *healing*. A Hope Restored® marriage intensive can provide you with personalized, biblically based support to help you put the pieces of your marriage back together.

Learn more at: **HopeRestored.com**
or call **1-866-875-2915**

HOPE RESTORED®
A Marriage Intensive Experience